HOW THE
BODY
OF CHRIST
TALKS

HOW THE
BODY
OF CHRIST
TALKS

Recovering the Practice
of Conversation in the Church

C. CHRISTOPHER SMITH

BrazosPress
a division of Baker Publishing Group
Grand Rapids, Michigan

© 2019 by C. Christopher Smith

Published by Brazos Press
a division of Baker Publishing Group
PO Box 6287, Grand Rapids, MI 49516-6287
www.brazospress.com

Printed in the United States of America

Library of Congress Cataloging-in-Publication Data
Names: Smith, C. Christopher, author.
Title: How the body of Christ talks : recovering the practice of conversation in the Church / C. Christopher Smith.
Description: Grand Rapids : Brazos Press, 2019. | Includes bibliographical references.
Identifiers: LCCN 2018036385 | ISBN 9781587434112 (pbk. : alk. paper)
Subjects: LCSH: Conversation—Religious aspects—Christianity. | Dialogue.
Classification: LCC BV4597.53.C64 S65 2019 | DDC 250—dc23
LC record available at https://lccn.loc.gov/2018036385

ISBN 978-1-58743-432-7 (casebound)

In keeping with biblical principles of creation stewardship, Baker Publishing Group advocates the responsible use of our natural resources. As a member of the Green Press Initiative, our company uses recycled paper when possible. The text paper of this book is composed in part of post-consumer waste.

19 20 21 22 23 24 25   7 6 5 4 3 2 1

green
press
INITIATIVE

That peoples can no longer carry on authentic dialogue with one another is not only the most acute symptom of the pathology of our time, it is also that which most urgently makes a demand of us.

—Martin Buber, *Pointing the Way*

The living human community that language creates involves living human bodies. We need to talk *together*, speaker and hearer here, now. We know that. We feel it. We feel the absence of it.

Speech connects us so immediately and vitally because it is a physical, bodily process, to begin with.

—Ursula K. Le Guin,
The Wave in the Mind

Contents

Introduction

We Are Conversational Bodies

More than one scientist has expressed frustration with how little is known about the *organization* of our biological faculties, functioning with such an integrated degree of coordination that we are capable of what would seem to be mental and physical miracles.

—Sherwin Nuland, *The Wisdom of the Body*

It's no secret that many churches today are struggling. Much has been written about the exodus of millennials from church life, but this exodus is broader, cutting across all generations. "Americans are attending church less," notes the Barna Group, which tracks trends within Christianity, "and more people are experiencing and practicing their faith outside of its four walls."[1] The force of individualism runs rampant not only in Western culture but also in our theology; it forms in us the sense that one can be a Christian and not be part of a church.

One of the most acute pains that prompts the exit of church members is the sense that they don't belong. Church members may feel that they are invisible or that some of their deepest convictions

1

are not being heard or taken seriously. This invisibility, if it persists, will eventually trigger the response, "You lost me." (This sentiment is the title of a 2011 book by David Kinnaman exploring this phenomenon.) Although Kinnaman's book focuses on millennials and other younger Christians, the exodus is bigger than that. People of socially and theologically conservative convictions leave churches that are becoming more progressive. People of socially and theologically progressive convictions leave conservative churches. People of older generations leave churches that are enamored with youthfulness. Young people leave churches that seem resistant to adapting to the times. Many people want to follow Jesus but increasingly feel like they are being forced out of churches where they don't belong—hence, we see the rise of those who see themselves as "spiritual but not religious."

We didn't realize the full effects of what we were doing at the time, but over twenty years ago my own congregation, Englewood Christian Church, located on the urban Near Eastside of Indianapolis, created a space in which the convictions of our members could be spoken and explored, and in which we began to know one another more fully. In the mid-1990s, our church had a Sunday evening worship service that was rapidly dying off, but we didn't want to give up being together on Sunday nights. Someone suggested that we gather on Sunday nights for conversation about our faith in Christ. So we gathered and awkwardly tried to talk together, but we rapidly realized how deeply we had been formed by a culture that has little capacity for conversation. Our early conversations together were a hot mess: people sometimes yelled at each other and often were deeply sarcastic; some people left the church altogether; others remained in the church but steered clear of our Sunday night conversations. Maybe it was stubbornness that kept us going, but we persisted in conversation on Sunday nights—week after week, month after month, year after year—and we gradually found that we were coming to know and trust one another and, in the process, were maturing in our capacity for conversation.

At the same time, we began to see conversations popping up in other parts of our life together, not just on Sunday nights. We have started a handful of businesses over the past decade or so, and those brought with them their own sorts of conversations and questions: How do we do the work well and faithfully as a community of Christ followers? How do we partner well with other groups who are doing similar work in our neighborhood and beyond? How do we do this work in a way that is increasingly sustainable and just, both for our employees and for our customers?

We also found ourselves drawn into vital conversations about the health and future of our neighborhood, and we were prepared to contribute significantly to these conversations because we had years of experience navigating the tensions of conversation as a church. Conversation has become a way of life for us over the past two decades. Our life together is often slow and messy (more on that in chap. 6), but our many interconnected conversations over the years seem to be leading us into deeper presence with one another and deeper into the compassionate way, truth, and life of Jesus. As the body of Christ, we are learning what it means to belong to one another and to work together, just as all the parts of the human body belong to one another and work together for the health and growth of that body.

Our bodies, created in the image of the Triune God, have much to teach us about the virtues of conversation. The human body is a wondrous symphony of diverse parts: 206 bones and over 600 muscles, controlled by more than a billion neurons and energized by 60,000 miles of veins and arteries in the circulatory system, enough to circle the globe twice. These intricate parts work together in a harmonious conversation, mobilizing our body and striving for its health. Our bodies constantly adapt to instabilities among their members. When I trip over a curb, for instance, my body tries to adjust itself and regain my balance. If that doesn't work, it will in an instant adjust its members to break my fall and cause as little damage as possible. When my body is thrown into instability by an infection, the lymphatic system works around the clock to fight the infection and restore the body's stability. Instabilities like these are not merely exceptional cases; to walk, for example, is to fall and repeatedly catch oneself. Similarly, our bodies are constantly fighting toxins that enter through the air we breathe or the food we eat, and the overwhelming majority of these skirmishes go unnoticed by us. In order for systems and body parts to work together successfully in these ways, the body maintains a complex, constant conversation among its parts; information and needs circulate and are refined and adjusted as a result of this ongoing conversation. We exist in our flesh as a many-layered conversation that is not simply idle banter but that moves us toward stability, health, and action.

At the most basic level, the human body is a conversation among proteins that are absorbed by our cells or transferred from one cell to another. The emerging science of proteomics studies the dynamics of this conversation, but it is still developing the tools necessary to listen effectively to the conversation and track the changes and movements of the proteins within it. Researchers like Danny Hillis, a computer scientist who has developed some of the rudimentary tools of proteomics, are hopeful that by better understanding the conversation unfolding at the protein level, we can better describe how diseases like cancer operate. Cancer is a breakdown, Hillis notes, "at the level of this conversation that's going on between the cells, that somehow the cells are deciding to divide when they shouldn't, not telling each other to die, or telling each other to make blood vessels when they shouldn't, or telling each other lies."[2] Indeed, it seems that the health of our bodies is intimately tied to the ability of their members to effectively converse together.

Our nervous system is perhaps the most familiar example of the way in which the human body is a conversation. Neurons, the cells that comprise the extensive network of our nervous system, have been specifically created for conversation. In a shape similar to that of a tree with both its branches and its roots, a neuron has dendrites on one end that resemble the tree's branches. These dendrites serve to receive input from a host of other neurons. The dendrites converge in the soma at what would be the top of the tree's trunk. The soma compiles the input from all the dendrites into one final signal. This signal is passed from the soma to the axons, which resemble the roots of the tree and serve to pass the neuron's signal on to other neurons. The synapses are the conversational space in which information is passed from the axons of one neuron to the dendrites of another.

Our bodies move and act through the ceaseless conversation that is unfolding through this vast network of neurons. Sensory data is passed at light speed from the exterior of the body to the brain, and the brain is constantly processing and discerning this data, sending instructions to all the parts of the body. Our muscles, tendons, ligaments, and bones are set in motion in harmony with this intricate conversation that is constantly rippling through our nervous system.

Our bodies are a multilayered conversation carried on internally, among the various parts. But that is not the full story. We are also the product of, and situated within, conversations external to ourselves. We exist as the result of the intimate, sexual conversation of our biological parents,[3] and we are an extension of the conversations and the histories they embody. Our bodies are situated within particular genetic, cultural, and socioeconomic conversations. Specifically, we exist and function within places that have been formed (and continue to be formed) by a multidimensional conversation that includes law, science, language, mythology, geography, and other dimensions. Language is the medium for this conversation, but we are continually negotiating the meaning and usage of words over time. As we learn to speak and eventually to read, we are being immersed in this conversation and cannot escape the deeply conversational nature of reality. Language is not the only extension of social conversation; clothes, food, housing, and many other facets of life are also embedded in social conversations.

Within and without, we are conversational bodies, created to live most fully and most healthfully in conversation. It is in community—in the social bodies of church, family, and workplace, for example—that we learn what it means to belong to others and to a story that is bigger than ourselves. Although we may have close and intimate connections with others, we never belong merely to individual persons. Rather, we belong to social bodies. A marriage is a great illustration. When I married my wife, we joined ourselves not only to each other but also to each other's families. The social bodies to which we belong are most healthy when they have a high capacity for conversation and are able to discuss their identity, work through challenges, and envision their futures.

Sociologists have reminded us repeatedly over the past half century that many of our social bodies in the twenty-first century are far from healthy, as described in renowned books like Bill Bishop's *The Big Sort* (2008), Robert Putnam's *Bowling Alone* (2000), and *Habits of the Heart* (1985) by Robert Bellah and others. The individualism championed by Enlightenment philosophers in the seventeenth and eighteenth centuries has saturated Western culture and—together with other factors, including consumerism and an ever-accelerating pace of life—wreaked havoc on almost every sort of social body. Robert Putnam writes, "For the first two-thirds of the twentieth century a powerful tide bore Americans into even deeper engagement in the life of their communities, but a few decades ago—silently, without warning—that tide reversed and we were overtaken by a treacherous rip current. Without at first noticing, we have been pulled apart from one another and from our communities over the last third of a century."[4]

Bill Bishop describes one of the societal forces at work in the last quarter of the twentieth century as "the big sort," a shift in which the networks of people we interact with have become substantially more homogeneous.[5] Our neighbors, our coworkers, our fellow church members, he argues, are more likely to be of similar ethnic and socioeconomic backgrounds than they were fifty or more years ago. As our social networks become homogenized, we lose the capacity to talk, to work, and to be with those who are different from us. And Bishop's book was released in 2008, before the boom of social media, which has only amplified the homogenizing effects of the big sort over the last decade.

Regardless of where we sit on the ideological spectrum, it is difficult today to have conversations with those who locate themselves at a substantially different place on this spectrum. Those on the Left struggle to talk with those on the Right, and vice versa, and those who identify with neither Left nor Right are often castigated by both sides. Many people feel the awkwardness of our inability to converse in family gatherings, for instance, which sometimes feel like a field of landmines that we all tiptoe across, trying to avoid those topics in the news or in our neighborhoods that are sure to explode if we misstep.

Our churches often are not much better. We file in, worship, perhaps chitchat over coffee, and then file out. We rarely have meaningful, sustained conversations with the sisters and brothers in our congregations. We read familiar passages about being the body of Christ, about bearing one another's burdens, and even about loving our enemies, but we have little imagination for how to *embody* these convictions in the everyday lives of our church communities. And yet, the situation of our churches should not come as much of a surprise. We are formed by the forces of a culture in which belonging to social bodies has ebbed, and in which we—often without realizing it—sort ourselves into spaces where most of the people are of similar backgrounds to us. The cumulative effect of these social forces is that we are being formed with a diminished capacity for conversation, and we bring this resistance to conversation with us as we gather in our churches.

Just as cancer is a breakdown in the human body's ability to adequately converse among its members, so too our inability to talk together in our churches, and especially to talk with people of different ages and backgrounds, is a cancerous disease that erodes our congregational health and threatens the future of our faith. Recognizing that we belong to one another in Christ's body, our health and our future depend on our ability to learn to talk and work together as the members of our human bodies do. The fundamental question that I wrestle with in this book, therefore, is: How do we learn to talk together in our churches when we have been formed by a culture that goes to great lengths to avoid conversation?

You may wonder, why *churches*? Shouldn't we learn to talk together in our homes, our neighborhoods, and our workplaces? Yes, of course we can and should continue to hone our conversational skills in all the communities to which we belong. But in the church we are provided with the scriptural story, which—as I will explain in the next chapter—offers us an account of *how* and *why* we belong to God and to one another and thus why our capacity for conversation should be one of the church's defining marks. It is in our churches, I believe, that we learn how to talk well with others. Our practices of forgiveness and reconciliation, for instance, create a space in which we can toddle and fall repeatedly as we are learning how to talk together.

Following in the way of Jesus, we learn to set aside our personal agendas and to seek the common good of our sisters and brothers and that of our place. As we mature together in our capacity for healthy conversation in our churches, we will find ourselves increasingly capable of patient and compassionate conversation in our homes, neighborhoods, and beyond. In a world where the pace of life seems to be ever-accelerating, I am hopeful that our churches can be communities that embody a different way, one in which we slow down, gather our hearts and minds together, and discern thoughtful, creative, and compassionate ways to respond to the situations in which we find ourselves.

Our human bodies bear witness to the deep correlation between belonging and conversation. If we understand ourselves as belonging to a body, we should be willing to have the conversations necessary for the health of that body—even if they prove to be painful. At the same time, conversation is crucial to the sort of discovery by which we discern the identity of the body to which we belong and thus become more confident in our sense of belonging to it. As babies, we go through a phase of discovering our senses and discovering that the parts of our bodies are connected to one another. We learn, for instance, that we can touch nearby things that we see, or that things we touch and move into our mouths with our hands can be tasted. This journey of discovery never ends. We learn with time that our bodies can do all sorts of things—talk with other bodies, paint pictures, write sentences, sing, dance, climb mountains—and with enjoyment and repetition, our identity is constantly refined and all the parts of our body slowly learn the skills required to mature into that identity. In her book *Braving the Wilderness*, Brené Brown explores what it means to belong to a community. "True belonging is not passive," she writes. "It's not the belonging that comes with just joining a group. It's not fitting in or pretending or selling out because it's safer. It's a practice that requires us to be vulnerable, get uncomfortable, and learn how to be present with people without sacrificing who we are. We want true belonging, but it takes tremendous courage to knowingly walk into hard moments."[6]

What I offer in this book is a field guide of sorts for the journey toward belonging—a treacherous journey, no doubt, in an age when the terrain is so unfamiliar. Like Abram, called out of the land of his ancestors, or the Israelites, led out of Egypt into the wilderness, we don't know where this journey is headed or what kinds of turns we will take along the way, but we have a sense of who God is, our call to be God's people, and a promise that God will bless and heal us. I have spent the last quarter century wandering this terrain: uprooting myself from family and church to go to college five hundred miles away from home, then discerning a call to live in Christian community after college, and eventually landing here at Englewood Christian Church, a community on this journey of learning to talk together and belong to one another in Christ.

My convictions about the transformative power of conversation that begins in our local church communities have emerged and are continually being formed by my own participation for over fifteen years in the conversational life of Englewood. A variety of stories from Englewood's journey, as well as those of other churches that are also learning to talk together, are interwoven throughout this book.

After an initial chapter that provides some orientation for our journey from the scriptural story—reminding ourselves of who God is and who we have been created to be as humans in God's image—the remainder of the book is divided into three parts. The first of these parts, "Setting Out on the Journey," offers some wisdom for churches that desire to begin practicing conversation. In the second part, "A Spirituality for the Journey," I identify three other practices that will help members of our churches converse better with one another. In the third and final part of the book, "Sustaining the Journey," I explore how we can keep growing and moving on this journey, even in the face of threats like tedium and conflict.

One of our deepest human desires is to belong. God, our Creator and Sustainer, has provided in the people of God a channel through which this desire might be fulfilled, a school in which we learn the virtues that we need to become healthy and Christlike communities. Although we find joy and fulfillment in belonging to healthy and maturing churches, our end is something bigger: a witness to the world of the loving and just character of God and of the hope of belonging.

1

Orienting Ourselves for the Journey

Theological Roots of Conversation

God's very nature is to be in dialogue: [the Trinity] in an eternal movement or flow of openness and receiving, a total giving and accepting, spilling over into creation and calling creation back into communion with Godself.

—Stephen Bevans and Roger Schroeder,
Prophetic Dialogue

Our bodies are always situated within larger conversations and larger stories. The world didn't begin with me or you, and I suspect that it will not end with us either. According to the scriptural story, even the first humans were created from other preexisting materials, as part of God's story of creation. We are creatures in God's story, and we function best when we are guided and oriented by our knowledge of who God is and of the story of God's action in creation.

The fundamental question this book addresses is, How can our churches initiate and sustain practices of conversation? But before we turn to this central question, it will be beneficial for us to look first at the questions of who God is and what God is doing in the world, as these questions will highlight *why* conversation is vital both to who we are as human beings created in God's image and to the work of reconciliation that God is doing in creation.

The Mystery of the Trinity

Over the past half century, theologians have increasingly recognized that our conversational existence as humans is at the core of our being as people created in the image of the Triune God, who exists as three-in-one, an eternal conversation characterized by love, presence, and cooperation. The Trinity is one of the greatest mysteries of the Christian faith. It defies our rationality. How can God be both one and three?[1] Philosophers and theologians have grappled with the nature of the Trinity since the earliest centuries of the church. One prominent, longstanding interpretation of the Trinity, social trinitarianism, emphasizes the three divine persons, in contrast to other interpretations that emphasize their unity. Social trinitarians maintain that God is fundamentally a social being and that humankind created in God's image is also fundamentally social. This social account of the Trinity offers us a depiction of God-in-conversation—that is, God invites us into a life of conversation not only with God but also with our fellow human beings.

As we prepare to reflect on the discipline of conversation, I want to highlight three facets of the relationship among the persons of the Trinity. Following the theology of social trinitarianism, I believe that careful reflection on the nature and the relationships of the Trinity will illuminate the ways we seek to live faithfully in community with other human beings. Although there are many facets of the Trinity that could be explored, I will focus on three:

mutual presence, an economy of reciprocity, and the way in which the Trinity is bound together in diversity.

Mutual Presence

Theologians who take a social view of the Trinity often describe the unity of the three divine persons in terms of their "indwelling" of one another. To say that the persons of the Trinity indwell one another is also to say that they are mutually present to one another. In mutual presence, the persons of the Trinity are fully attentive to one another, speaking and responding out of this complete attentiveness. In addressing the Jews who were upset that Jesus healed on the Sabbath, Jesus responded that

> the Son can do nothing on his own, but only what he sees the Father doing: for whatever the Father does, the Son does likewise. The Father loves the Son and shows him all that he himself is doing. . . . Just as the Father raises the dead and gives them life, so also the Son gives life to whomever he wishes. . . . I can do nothing on my own. As I hear, I judge; and my judgment is just, because I seek to do not my own will but the will of him who sent me. (John 5:19–21, 30)

This link between the words, the being, and the actions of the Trinity is also reiterated in John 14. Philip asks to see the Father, and Jesus insists that Philip has already seen the Father in Jesus himself: "Whoever has seen me has seen the Father. How can you say, 'Show us the Father'? Do you not believe that I am in the Father and the Father is in me? The words that I say to you I do not speak on my own; but the Father who dwells in me does his works. Believe me that I am in the Father and the Father is in me; but if you do not, then believe me because of the works themselves" (John 14:9–11). Later in the same admonition to Philip, Jesus emphasizes that he will ask the Father to send the Spirit to live among his disciples, and the Spirit will come and abide with them and live in them (v. 17). The role of the Spirit is to guide

13

Christ's followers "into all the truth; for he will not speak on his own, but will speak whatever he hears" (16:13).

Later in this chapter, we will flesh out the ways God desires to be present with humanity. Our bodies, created in the image of the Triune God, reflect the mutual presence of the Trinity. The members of a fully mature and fully healthy human body are mutually present to one another and act according to their presence with one another. The action of my hand, for instance, flows from its response to the messages that are passed to it via the nervous system, in accord with the action of the arm and shoulder to which it is attached. My hand does not do anything apart from the conversation and action of my body as a whole. If my hand were injured, the rest of my body would respond to protect and heal it, allowing it to rest, fighting infection with white blood cells, and so forth.

Our local churches, manifestations of Christ's body in our particular places, are similarly intended to be social bodies in which one crucial marker of health and maturity is members who are mutually present to one another. The L'Arche communities—founded in 1964 by Jean Vanier as places where "people with and without intellectual disabilities live and work together as peers"[2]—are a good example of faith communities in which all members are learning to be mutually present to one another. Often the core members of L'Arche communities (those who have a disability) are not able to communicate with words but instead speak through motions or emotions. Noncore members have to be present and attentive over time in order to learn to communicate with core members. Communication cannot be taken for granted; it is hard work that is cultivated day-by-day as all members of a L'Arche community live together and care for one another. Journalist Kristin Lin spent some time with L'Arche communities and articulates this work well:

> I've come of age in the world of words; I believe in their power to connect, even redeem, us. I take faith—comfort—in their ability

to frame, account, order, justify. But I think I've forgotten (or never knew) the value of *not* knowing what to say, or even what to think, or do—the value of simply *being*—and being accepted for just that. . . . Presence is difficult, and L'Arche members seemed acutely aware of the uncertainty and awkwardness and hurt that comes with it. The gifts of presence are not always found in the comforts of getting along with each other, but rather in sitting with messiness and complexity.[3]

Both core and noncore L'Arche members regularly find that they are being transformed by their mutual presence with one another. Vanier tells the story of a woman who came to a L'Arche community in her early forties. This woman was epileptic and paralyzed on one side of her body. When she arrived, she was prone to frequent violent outbursts, but as she continued for months and years as part of L'Arche, being cared for and accepted for who she was, she slowly began to be transformed and the violence began to ebb.[4] Similarly, noncore members of L'Arche have reported being transformed by their presence with core members, learning patience, tenderness, and unconditional love.

An Economy of Reciprocity

Any community will necessarily have an economy, a flow of resources that is an expression of care for its members. Although we would err to say that any person of the Trinity has need of anything, resources are freely shared in the caring triune community that is God. Jesus acknowledges several times in the Gospel accounts that everything he has comes from the Father (e.g., Matt. 11:27). As the Spirit descended on the followers of Jesus in Jerusalem on the day of Pentecost, one of the characteristics of the life that they found in the Spirit is captured in the Greek word *koinōnia* (Acts 2:42), and similarly in this life that flows from the Spirit: "There was not a needy person among them" (4:34).

Our human bodies function by an economy of reciprocity through, for instance, the processes of metabolism and respiration. In the alveoli and the capillaries, oxygen is taken from the air and infused into the blood; at the same time, carbon dioxide goes in the opposite direction, from the blood to the air. In metabolism, food is changed into energy that the body needs for action. In the economy of our bodies, these needed resources flow freely to the members who need them. Our bodies, of course, are not a self-contained system. Through respiration and metabolism we take in substances that originated in other creatures. Plants and animals become life and energy for us in our food. Similarly, oxygen created through the photosynthesis of plants and trees flows through our lungs and circulates through our bodies, giving us life. In these ways, our bodies reflect the free-flowing economy of the Trinity.

Hospitality, for instance, is a practice through which our churches create spaces in which this economy of reciprocity can flourish. In her landmark book on Christian hospitality, *Making Room*, Christine Pohl describes Christian communities that have sought to live in solidarity with the poor, noting that "hospitality offers a model for developing more reciprocal relationships."[5] One of the most striking stories of Christian hospitality in the last century is the Reformed Church in Le Chambon, France, led by André and Magda Trocmé, who guided their community to shelter thousands of Jews escaping Nazi Germany. The people of Le Chambon not only opened their homes, schools, and churches to the Jews and helped them create illicit paperwork that could save their lives but were also present and in conversation with their guests. They did not look down on the Jews in their tragic circumstances but saw them as equals and worked to find opportunities for their gifts to be employed in the life and work of the town.

Richard Unsworth, biographer of the Trocmés, describes two particular Jews who were given the opportunity to work in Le Chambon: Madame Berthe, who served as a helper for Magda, and Monsieur Colin, a cabinetmaker who was originally from

Berlin and built furniture for households in Le Chambon.[6] These stories gesture toward the economy of reciprocity that began to take shape in this French town as Christian hospitality was extended toward the Jews. The Jewish refugees were not merely the recipients of resources; they also were given the opportunity to work and contribute to the life and economy of Le Chambon. The Christian hospitality embodied in Le Chambon reminds us of the life of the Trinity: God is a community of persons, a community that is open to humankind in all our woundedness and immaturity, making a space for us to participate in and contribute to the reign of God on earth as it is in heaven.

Bound Together in Diversity

A crucial tenet in understanding the Trinity, according to orthodox Christian theology, is that "Father, Son, and Holy Spirit are not identical."[7] The Trinity thus consists of three persons bound into one, through their indwelling of one another. We see in the scriptural story that the three persons of the Trinity have distinct roles and functions: the Son took on flesh and lived as a human being in first-century Palestine; the Holy Spirit came among the gathering of Jesus's followers at Pentecost and continues to abide with and guide God's people today; the Father, enthroned in the heavens, is the divine mystery, the source of all creation.

Yet despite their diversity, the three persons of the Trinity are one, indwelling one another, each bearing witness to the others in their particular work. Indwelling allows the three persons to be bound without coercion; each member remains free. Our human bodies reflect the nature of the Trinity, as a community of diverse members bound together. Each body part has its own function and yet relies on the body as a whole. One part of the body is free to perform its function or not, but because it is indwelled by other parts of the body, the one thing it cannot do is leave the body of its own volition. One or both of my eyes might go blind, for instance, but they cannot choose to leave my body. The body as a whole may choose to act together to pluck out an eye (or two), but this is a coordinated action of the mind, the hand, the arm, and so forth, and the body will suffer as a result of this choice. Unlike our bodies, God is defined by love and wholeness and would not choose to remove a member of the Trinity.

The history of the Christian tradition, beginning with the New Testament stories of Jews and gentiles being committed to each other in the earliest church communities, is full of stories of diverse people bound together in congregations—women and men, rich and poor, highly educated and uneducated, native peoples and foreigners—worshiping and working together in the same church community. Likewise today, amid the deeply broken racial history of the United States, some of the most striking stories of diverse people committed to one another can be seen in interracial churches. Chris Rice tells the story of one such church—the Antioch community in Jackson, Mississippi, in the 1980s—in his powerful book *Grace Matters*. Rice is frank about the many challenges of life together in this community, but he and other members were being transformed by their daily presence with one another in a neighborhood riddled with crime and poverty. He describes the experience and in particular his friendship with Spencer Perkins, one of the black leaders of the community: "It was not a gift I would have chosen, but maybe it was the gift that I needed."[8] Stories like this remind us that we have been created in the image of the Triune God, not merely to be in community but to be in community with those who differ from us.

God Desires to Be Present with Humanity

Just as the persons of the Trinity are mutually present to one another in conversation, so too, as the shape of Scripture's story from beginning to end reveals, does God desire to be present with humanity. God is present with Adam in the garden of Eden and is in conversation with him there. Given the social nature of the Trinity as described above, God deems that it is not good for Adam to be alone (Gen. 2:18), and so God creates the animals of the field and the birds of the air and invites Adam to name each one. God not only talks with Adam; God is also attentive to Adam's presence, recognizing his loneliness and the fact that even after the animals are created, Adam still lacks a helper and partner (v. 20). Thus Eve is created. Adam and Eve, male and female, are two distinct persons, yet both are created in the image of God.

In the garden of Eden, God and humans are present to one another and in conversation with one another, but this presence is shattered by human disobedience. One of the first consequences of the fall is that Adam and Eve "hid themselves from the presence of the LORD God" (Gen. 3:8). As a result of their infidelity to the life God had prepared for them in the garden, the humans are banished from the garden. Although God always desires and strives to be present with humankind, the human condition is marked thereafter by our efforts to hide ourselves from the presence of God. Our failure to abide in God's presence quickly devolves into violence, first in the story of Cain killing Abel, his brother, and then in the age of Noah, when "the earth was corrupt in God's sight, . . . filled with violence" (6:11). After the flood and the preservation of Noah and his family, God vows that humanity will never be wiped out by a flood again, and God works to establish a new way of being present to humankind—by dwelling among a particular people.

God makes a covenant with Abraham and abides with the descendants of Abraham, Isaac, and Jacob, speaking with them and guiding them. Human infidelity is marked throughout Israel's beginnings by people who hide from God's presence and who do what they prefer instead of what God asks of them. Indeed,

throughout the entire story of the Old Testament, Israel is am-
bivalent toward God's presence with them. Sometimes they honor
God's presence and follow God's guidance. Often though, they
reject God's presence and act as if they can guide and govern
themselves. One of the most powerful stories of this sort is that of
Israel rejecting God's presence and demanding a king, like those
the pagan nations around them had (1 Sam. 8). God tells Samuel
all the horrible things that will happen if Israel chooses to follow
a human king, but the Israelite people refuse to hear the wisdom
of Samuel and make up their minds to reject God's presence and
governance in favor of a human king.

Although Israel rejected God's kingship, God continued to
be present with them in the era of the kings in the temple that
King Solomon built. God's presence did not stay in the temple,
however. Ezekiel tells of how the temple in his day was full of
abominations—the Israelites worshiped foreign gods in the temple and filled the land with violence (Ezek. 8:17). God rebukes
Israel, and the presence of God is withdrawn from the temple.
After God's presence is gone, Israel is driven into exile and the
temple is destroyed by the army of the Babylonian king, Nebu-
chadnezzar. God does not intend, however, to abandon Israel
forever. Ezekiel records God's promise to make peace with Israel
and to restore the presence of God with them forever (37:26–27).
This promise would be fulfilled as God would eventually become
present with Israel in a new way, by taking on flesh and dwelling
among them.

Jesus, God incarnate, fulfilled God's promise to be Immanuel,
God-with-us. God took on flesh in Jesus of Nazareth and dwelled
with first-century Jews in Palestine, experiencing all the joys—for
instance, the wedding feast at Cana, where he turned water into
wine—and all the sorrows of the human experience, including
the death of his friend Lazarus. Jesus gathered a community of
disciples around himself, and day-by-day he ate and drank and
traveled with these friends. Being God, Jesus could have seen them

as servants, but he instead chose to call them friends (John 15:15). God's presence in Jesus is ultimately rejected by the masses, and Jesus is sentenced to die on a cross. Although he died and was buried, Jesus was resurrected on the third day, underscoring that God's presence with humanity cannot be killed off but will indeed abide with us until the end of time.

For a time after his resurrection, Jesus walks and eats with his disciples, and eventually he ascends into the heavens. Jesus emphasizes that the ascension is not a forsaking of his followers and that the Holy Spirit will come on them after he ascends. God will continue to guide the community of God's people through the Holy Spirit. At Pentecost, not long after the ascension, the Holy Spirit becomes present to Jesus's followers. The book of Acts is an account of God's people learning to be attentive to the Spirit's presence with them and of the ways that God guides them through controversies, through the inclusion of gentiles into God's people, and through the spread of the gospel to a large swath of the Mediterranean region.

A large chunk of the New Testament story consists of epistles— letters written by the apostles to churches throughout the Roman Empire—aimed at helping them discern and live faithfully with God's presence among them in the Holy Spirit. Our churches today are located within this story of God being present to and guiding local communities of God's people. Where is this story headed in which we are enmeshed? The end of the story, as told in the book of Revelation, is depicted as the whole earth living and acting faithfully with God's presence, a return to the conversational life for which we were created. The new creation, established in Jesus, has been completed; the old world of infidelity and rebellion is wiped away. Death is no more and life flows from God's very presence like a river, sustaining the whole of creation (Rev. 21:1–4). This eternal city that draws its light and life from God's presence is the flourishing, conversational life for which we were created!

The Church as Continuing Incarnation

Amid the deep fragmentation of the late modern world, we seem to be a long way from the fulfillment of this new creation built on God's presence with humankind. We find ourselves still in the thick of the scriptural story. Like the early Christians in the book of Acts, guided by the Spirit, we struggle with every fiber of our being to stay focused on the end of the story and to pay attention to how the Holy Spirit is already present with us and guiding us through the many particular challenges that we face in the twenty-first century.

I have long been fascinated by the apostle Paul's references to the temple of the Holy Spirit in 1 Corinthians (e.g., 6:19). The grammar of these references is often obscured by the quirks of the English language and the prevailing individualism of our modern age: "Your [plural] body [singular] is the temple of the Holy Spirit." In contrast to the convictions of popular theology, we are *not* wholly autonomous individuals who each bear the Holy Spirit within us. Rather, Paul seems to be saying that the Holy Spirit is present in the local gathering of God's people. First Corinthians was written to a particular church community in first-century Corinth, and therefore Paul seems to be referring to the body not as a universal and abstract entity but as a particular congregation of God's people situated in a particular time and place. Throughout Scripture, we learn that God's presence dwells primarily with the people of God. Apart from Jesus, the presence of God does not dwell *in* an individual in Scripture but rather is located in and with God's people.

Through this reading of Paul's epistle, we see that God's presence with our church communities in the Holy Spirit is not just for our guidance but also serves to bear witness to God's presence to our neighbors who regularly see and interact with us. In this way, we embody Christ—albeit immaturely and imperfectly—in ways that help our neighbors see and interact with God. Christ's body takes shape in our local community as we talk together and discern the particular ways the Spirit is present among us and ways God's presence with us guides us as we move forward.

Here at our church in Indianapolis, the covenant that gives shape to our life together describes our congregation as both "a manifestation of Christ in this location" and "a tangible presence of Christ in this place."⁹ In each of these expressions, we use the indefinite article ("a") instead of the definite article ("the") because there are other churches in our neighborhood that are also manifestations of Christ's body in this place. This grammar reminds us that no church—neither ours nor any other—is fully equivalent to Christ's presence. "The church can never control, but only submit to Christ's presence," writes David Fitch. "It is always a witness to Christ's presence, embodying it but never equivalent to it."¹⁰

By learning to talk together, to be present to one another, and to follow the guidance of Christ's presence with us in the Holy Spirit, we are maturing into the "full stature of Christ" (Eph. 4:13). As our churches mature, learning to talk and be present with one another, we discover the particular functions that each member has been prepared by the Holy Spirit to enact in the life of our church body. This life for which we have been prepared, and into which we have been called as God's people, is precisely the life of the Trinity, characterized by mutual presence, an economy of reciprocity, and a community of diverse persons bound together as one.

The Dialogue of Salvation

Conversation, as I describe it in this book, is a discipline through which we learn and practice the abundant life of God for which we were created. Earlier in this chapter, I described the relationships of the persons of the Trinity in terms of their mutual presence, their reciprocity, and their bond in diversity. As we are learning to talk together, we are learning to be present to one another, to give and receive from one another in the reciprocity of God's abundant economy, and to be committed to one another despite our diversity. Conversation is difficult for us as human beings. We have been shaped by histories of brokenness: of oppression due to poverty, race, gender, or ethnicity; of the national violence of war or the domestic violence of abuse; of greed that drives both oppression and violence. And these are only a handful of the causes at the heart of our profound brokenness. These histories compel us to withhold our presence from others out of fear—or, on the opposite extreme, to withhold our presence by manipulating others through authoritarian control. These histories incline us to resist sharing ourselves and our resources in reciprocity. They also make it difficult for us to stay committed to others, particularly those who differ from us.

Within this history of brokenness that goes back to the garden of Eden, we human beings are not well prepared to enter into and sustain a conversational life. Indeed, we will inevitably avoid and wound one another in our efforts to talk together. Although we should not intentionally try to inflict these wounds, we should recognize the opportunity that we are afforded in them to practice forgiveness, healing, and reconciliation.

The salvation into which we are invited in Jesus, as Dallas Willard has reminded us,[11] is a life. Specifically, it is a life in conversation with God, with the sisters and brothers of our local church communities, and with our neighbors. The love and grace to which we are called in Jesus make our local churches an ideal place to practice our conversational skills and to mature in them, but our conversations should also eventually spill over into our neighborhoods. Although the history of mission and evangelism in the Christian tradition has often been marked by manipulation and violence, our posture with our neighbors—and especially those who do not share our Christian faith—should be one of conversation.

"God, in an age-long dialogue, has offered and continues to offer salvation to humankind," writes the Pontifical Council for Inter-religious Dialogue. "In faithfulness to the divine initiative, the Church too must enter into a dialogue of salvation with all men and women."[12] The abundant life into which we have been called in Jesus (John 10:10), and into which we invite our neighbors, is one of conversation and presence, of knowing and being known. And yet, as I detailed in this book's introduction, conversation is extremely difficult for Westerners in the twenty-first century.

We Need Intentionality

God created humans to be conversational beings, but we have been formed by the powers of the modern age to resist conversation. In this context, we need spaces within the common life of our church communities where we endeavor to relearn the arts of conversation by undertaking the discipline of intentionally talking together. Like ancient Israel when they were led to construct the tabernacle, thus creating a space for God's presence to be known in their midst, our churches today can create conversational spaces in which God's presence can be known among us. I have found it helpful to think of conversation as a corporate spiritual discipline, like prayer or worship. Spiritual disciplines "all deeply and essentially involve bodily conditions and activities," writes Dallas Willard. "Thus they show us effectively how we can 'offer our bodies as living sacrifices, holy and acceptable unto God' and how our 'spiritual worship' (Rom. 12:1) really is inseparable from the offering up of our bodies in specific physical ways."[13]

Although someone may be innately gifted, say, as a pianist or a basketball player, she will not fulfill this end without hundreds or even thousands of hours of practice. Conversation is an essential discipline that helps us cultivate the sort of faithful presence for which we were created. Faithful presence, writes David Fitch, "is at the heart of what it means to be the people of God. This is the thing we do that we call church. This is how God changes the world."[14] Disciplines, Fitch argues, are essential to the work of embodying faithful presence in our communities: "[Disciplines] open up space for God to rearrange the world, starting in our social relationships. These disciplines invite us into what God is actually doing in the whole world."[15]

Given our formation in a fragmented world that has little capacity for conversation, we desperately need to practice the discipline of conversation in our local church communities in order to mature in the witness we bear to the conversational nature of the Triune God and the dialogue of salvation into which God has invited humanity. The remainder of this book will explore how our churches can initiate disciplines of conversation, how we can cultivate a Christian spirituality that will nourish the discipline of conversation, and how we can sustain practices of conversation in the face of powers that vehemently resist it.

PART 1

SETTING OUT ON THE JOURNEY

2

Learning the Dynamics
of Conversation

People are hard to hate close up.
Move in.

—Brené Brown,
Braving the Wilderness

I t's hard not to love babies, especially when they are in a good
mood. Babies are cuddly and cute; they learn to smile not
long after they are born. In the earliest weeks of life, babies
are learning to communicate with their parents and others and to
express what they want or need. They communicate most of their
needs by crying: the need for food, the need for sleep, or the need
for a clean diaper, for instance. Sometimes it is not clear, even to
the most attentive parents, why a baby is crying.

The earliest months of a baby's life are a crucial time of learning coordination. In this first stage of life, we learn to focus our
eyes, to coo, and to make sounds other than crying. We gradually
learn to control these sounds to mimic words, and then we begin

to make associations between the mimicked sounds and specific people or objects. All these forms of learning are functions of bodily coordination. A baby learns quickly that her hands and feet are part of her body and not only that she can see them with her eyes but also that she can move them, first in flailing and eventually in much more careful motions. A baby learns over time to feed herself and learns not only how to move various parts of her body but also how to move her whole body by crawling and later walking and running. All the ways infants learn are rooted in their growing realizations that their body parts are connected to one another and that they can converse with one another and learn to work together to do increasingly complex tasks.

Babies don't merely learn to mature on their own. They need guidance to help them discover the many connected parts of their body and how these parts can interact with the world around them. Parents offer this kind of guidance as they play with a baby: smiling, talking, holding hands and feet, and offering toys, for instance. An infant who does not regularly have these sorts of interactions with a parent or other caring adult will be delayed in her maturity, and this neglect may eventually lead to mental or physical harm. Throughout the story of the earliest churches that unfolds in the New Testament, these church bodies understand themselves as being led toward maturity by the Holy Spirit. Not only were the early churches ligamented together by "the unity of the Spirit in the bond of peace" (Eph. 4:3) but also their bodies were helped in maturing toward "the full stature of Christ" (v. 13) through the gifts the Spirit provided.

In spite of the Spirit's leading, a major challenge for the early churches was their immaturity. The church in Corinth, for instance, was chided by Paul for their lack of maturity (1 Cor. 3). The Corinthians were divided by their loyalties to various apostles, and they refused to work together as a mature body. If we are honest with ourselves, we will likely see a good deal of our own churches' immaturity reflected back to us in the story of the early Corinthian church. Our church bodies have a few actions that we can do pretty well: gather for worship, serve our neighbors occasionally, introduce our children and youth to some important biblical stories. But like the Corinthians, we are divided by our loyalties to political parties, to theological traditions, and to a variety of contemporary Christian leaders. (One can easily imagine a similar argument today: "I follow Tim Keller." "Well, I follow Rachel Held Evans," or "I follow Richard Foster," and so on.) In our immaturity, we don't know how to talk and work together well, and this severely limits the capacity of what our church bodies can do.

Any sort of action that an infant learns is accomplished through practice, by repeating the action over and over until she can do it effortlessly. While it is easy to see and understand the external dynamics of an infant's actions, picking up a tiny piece of cereal and putting it in her mouth, for instance, we rarely stop to consider all the internal coordination and conversation between body parts that enable a particular action.

Just as a healthy baby eventually learns that her body parts are connected to one another and can communicate among themselves, so too it is valuable for our churches to understand the dynamics of conversation if we desire to mature into healthy, communicative bodies. Some of the most important dynamics of conversation are

1. the size of the group,
2. the degree of homogeneity in the group, and
3. the virtues and challenges of formal and informal conversations.

Group Size

The size of a conversation group can have a significant impact on how the conversation is perceived. A conversation between only two people is a very intimate one; each conversant has only one person on whom to focus and can devote herself and her attention solely to the other conversant. Conversation in pairs tends either to go really well, if the conversants connect well with each other, or to go really poorly, if one or both conversants struggle to connect and make conversation. For every new conversant added to the conversation, the complexity increases dramatically. While a group of three contains three two-person relationships, a group of twelve contains sixty-six two-person relationships. Given the escalating complexity as groups grow in number, some researchers have suggested that the optimum size of a conversation group is five to seven people.[1]

Conversation is not impossible in larger groups, but the ability for all conversants to participate fully and to pay close attention to all other participants declines as the size of the group grows. It's not so difficult for us to follow the verbal flow of conversation in a larger group, as long as everyone exercises respect and speaks one at a time. More challenging, though, is following both the verbal and the nonverbal flow, as conversants are constantly responding nonverbally, making it difficult for each person to follow the words and unspoken messages from every other person in the large group. As the size of the group stretches above twenty or thirty, it is easy for people in the group to become anonymous, mere observers of the conversation instead of participants. Conversation in larger groups tends to be carried by extroverts or other talkative ones who feel comfortable speaking in a group of that size. Good facilitation, which we will explore later in this chapter, can help to keep the group largely engaged in the conversation.

Degree of Homogeneity

One of the greatest challenges we face amid the fragmentation of the twenty-first century is learning to talk with those of different backgrounds than our own. Our language is largely a function of the cultures in which we were raised. Not only do we speak a particular language; we also use particular terms and expressions that reflect the people and places among which we learned to speak.

Unspoken modes of communication are also a product of our personal formation. While visiting several churches in Minnesota and hearing about their practices of conversation, the cultural dynamic of "Minnesota nice" kept popping up—a superficial niceness that appears pleasant, even in the face of matters about which people deeply disagree. Other people, in contrast, do not hesitate to put everything out on the table and aren't afraid to speak frankly about things they don't agree with. These culturally ingrained habits of how we talk together can complicate conversation, especially if we don't pay attention to them.

Although we may find it easier to talk with people who share similar cultural backgrounds (the nature of this similarity will vary in different settings—at times it is easier for us to talk with people of the same age, at other times people of the same ethnicity, and so on), communication research indicates that groups with different perspectives and skills are generally more productive than homogeneous ones.[2] Following the biblical wisdom of the apostle Paul, if every member of a body were an eye, we would have no hearing (1 Cor. 12:17). Thankfully, our human bodies do not consist solely of eyes (or toes or elbows). Rather, our bodies consist of many diverse parts that, as we mature, learn to talk and work together. Ideally, a conversation group will have both some homogeneity (language is a good example, as bilingual conversations are very difficult to sustain) and some heterogeneity that helps broaden our perspective and teaches us to listen and be sympathetic to those who are different. To return to the body metaphor, although the parts of our body are diverse, they communicate in a single, neurological language.

33

Formal versus Informal Conversations

A final dynamic to be attentive to as we learn to talk better together is the distinction between formal and informal conversations. Both of these modes of conversation can be vital to the life and flourishing of a community. In the previous chapter, I argued that churches in the twenty-first century need to practice conversation intentionally. This practice of learning to talk and listen together is one type of formal conversation, a gathering specifically for the purpose of conversation on a particular topic. Formal conversations should be a regular part of our approach to practicing conversation as a church. Informal conversations are those spontaneous ones that arise around the coffeepot or as we share meals with one another. Informal conversations are not guided by a specific topic or question; we simply talk together, sharing stories and things that are on our minds.

Both formal and informal conversations can help us learn to talk better together. One of the biggest differences between the two is that without some intentionality, our informal conversations tend to happen with people who are very similar to us. Without paying attention to what we are doing, most of the people we seek out for informal conversation—those we invite to go out to lunch or invite over to our homes, for example—are similar enough to us that we can be comfortable together. Formal conversation, however, creates a space in which we can learn to talk with heterogeneous others.

We need both formal and informal conversations; each type of conversation can help us talk more openly and compassionately in the other type of conversation. On the one hand, informal conversations provide a safe space in which we can be more vulnerable and begin to test the trust of others. Opening up in this way can help us cultivate the trust we need to be more open in formal conversations. On the other hand, formal conversations can help us learn to talk with those who differ from us and may, over time, open us up to informal conversations with those we might never have imagined that we would call friends. In formal conversation, we learn to be patient with one another and to work through differences of terminology, theological understanding, verbal and nonverbal expressions, and many other factors of conversation. This work—and indeed it is difficult and often draining work—will transform us and will likely change the dynamics of our informal conversations. For instance, we may seek out people of different ages, ethnicities, or education for informal conversation as a result of learning to talk with and appreciate them in our formal conversations.

Improving Our Conversational Dynamics

Ultimately, every community will have to discern how it is going to talk together. I cannot offer a single set of rules that will magically help all communities increase their capacity for conversation. Devoting our attention to a few specific factors, however, can make a major difference in the development of our conversational skills. The first of these factors is creating a space for regular, formal conversation in which we intentionally practice conversation as a congregation in all our diversity. Hopefully this space is not the only one in which we are talking to one another, and ideally we *will* indeed have other spaces where we are talking informally together.

To understand the importance of formal conversation, consider the example of a musician, let's say a guitar player. This guitarist may play the instrument in lots of places throughout the course of a week. She might play at home as a means of relaxation; she might play a few songs in a coffee shop; she might play at her church or in the park. But unless she takes some time for practicing new songs or chords, she is not going to grow or mature in her skills as a guitarist. Playing familiar songs over and over will likely help our guitarist play those songs really well, but it won't help her expand her repertoire. Formal conversation is similarly an important means by which we expand our conversational repertoire, learning to talk with others whose backgrounds differ greatly from our own or learning to talk about things that make us uncomfortable because they are unfamiliar or require us to be vulnerable.

Our formal conversations should be held regularly, just as one would expect to practice regularly as a musician or athlete, but the exact frequency of our formal conversations may vary— ideally somewhere between weekly and monthly. Having formal conversations together less than once a month creates a gap between each conversation in which we might be likely to forget the conversational skills we are learning. On the other end of the spectrum though, I cannot see much benefit in meeting for formal conversation more than once a week (except perhaps in the very occasional situation where a pressing question arises that simply must be resolved and the congregation has the momentum and desire to meet more than once a week). In the next chapter, I will consider the types of questions we might explore together in our formal conversations, especially as we are just beginning to practice talking together.

How we arrange ourselves for conversation is another factor that can make a big difference in the quality of our conversations. Arrange seats in a circle, oval, or other round shape that allows all participants to easily see one another. Given that so much of our communication is nonverbal, being able to see one another as well as possible helps us communicate better. Depending on the size of the group and the meeting space available, a circle might not be possible. A seating arrangement of concentric circles—although more inhibiting than a single circle—is a decent alternative when space is tight. The tighter the circle, the greater the likelihood that participants are able to see and hear one another. Pews, however, or any other linear arrangement in which participants are mostly looking at the backs of others' heads, are *not* conducive to good conversation. Similarly, the acoustics of a room can make a big difference in the quality of conversations. Cavernous rooms that don't absorb sound or that echo can inhibit our ability to hear one another and talk well together, especially for those who might have some degree of hearing impairment.

Facilitation

Another important factor in improving the dynamics of our conversations is good facilitation, the work of keeping the group on track, focused on our goals and pursuing them in the manner we have agreed on. Roger Schwarz, author of *The Skilled Facilitator*, writes, "The facilitator's main task is to help the group increase effectiveness by improving its process and structure. *Process* refers to how a group works together. It includes how members talk to each other, how they identify and solve problems, how they make decisions, and how they handle conflict. *Structure* refers to stable, recurring group process, examples being group membership or group roles."[3] If the group has ground rules (a topic we will discuss in the next chapter), the facilitator makes sure members stick to these rules. If the group is exploring a particular topic or question, the facilitator makes sure the conversation doesn't wander too far off topic. If the conversation seems to be fizzling out prematurely, the facilitator might ask some new yet pertinent questions to stoke the fire of the conversation. At the start of a gathering, the facilitator will introduce the question or topic to be discussed and, if the conversation is being continued from a previous gathering, will briefly refresh the group's memory of the earlier conversation.

Facilitation works best when the person serving as facilitator is as neutral as possible. Some experts on facilitation even recommend that a facilitator be someone from outside the group, but in most congregational settings, bringing in an outside facilitator simply isn't a reasonable expectation. Perhaps as a congregation is beginning to have conversations together, they might bring in an outside facilitator for a brief period of time to help them get started, but in the long term, a church should expect to provide its own facilitation. An internal facilitator has knowledge of a group that could take months or years for an external facilitator to develop. Such knowledge is essential for reading the group and guiding the group in its conversations. Neutrality does not mean that a facilitator has no opinions on the conversational topic. Rather, a neutral facilitator, writes Schwarz, facilitates "the discussion without sharing [her] opinions and so that the group members cannot tell what [she thinks] about the groups issues; consequently [the facilitator does] not influence the group's decisions."[4]

One thing we have learned through our church's two decades of Sunday night conversation is that it is preferable to have a team of facilitators who can take turns doing the work of facilitation, rather than a single facilitator who always functions in that role. For the first fifteen or so years of our conversations, we had one facilitator whose personality was a bit stoic, so he was generally quite good at practicing neutrality. We hadn't, however, done much study or reflection on good conversational process, so we didn't necessarily value neutrality, and our facilitator occasionally contributed to the conversation. The group tended to defer to these contributions in ways that it didn't defer to the contributions of nonfacilitators. Once we came to this realization, we decided to shift to a team of facilitators who could arrange a rotating schedule. On the weeks when they weren't serving in the facilitator role, they could contribute as normal participants in the conversation. But on the weeks they were assigned to facilitate, they tried to remain neutral, taking care not to interject their personal thoughts into the conversation. It has been beneficial for us not only to recognize and practice the virtues of neutral facilitation but also to have a small array of people—including young people—who are learning the skills of facilitation.

A major component of the work of facilitation is paying attention to and diagnosing the behavior of the group. A facilitator must be attuned to the verbal and nonverbal ways each person participates in the conversation. Beyond simply observing, the facilitator infers meaning from the behaviors she sees (e.g., someone who appears to be getting angry or drawing unnecessary attention to him- or herself). On the basis of these inferences, the facilitator must decide whether to intervene and how and why intervention is necessary. Healthy intervention begins with the facilitator describing the behavior that led to the intervention and asking the group whether they observed the same behavior in the same way. If the group agrees with the facilitator's observation, the facilitator should share her inference about what the behavior might mean and briefly touch on her rationale and intent for intervening. If the facilitator's observations appear to be correct, then the facilitator might make a suggestion or two about how the offending members could change their behaviors to better contribute to the group's conversation. The aim of intervention should never be to shame or punish conversants but always to sustain and cultivate the health of the conversation.[5]

A crucial part of observing the behavior of a conversation group is learning to read emotions. We have been created as humans, with emotions as part of our being, and we should not expect to set aside these emotions as we gather for conversation. Many of us in the twenty-first century, however, have been formed to suppress our emotions and do not know how to express them well or how to interpret them in the people around us. This malformation can complicate the work of the facilitator, but good facilitators either have an intuitive sense of how to read emotions or acquire this skill with practice.

Emotions may be difficult to express and read, but they are nonetheless a significant force within any conversation. Our emotions might be stirred by a particular topic of conversation, by tense relationships in the group (typically extending beyond the conversational time), by past experiences that relate to the topic of conversation, by misjudgments or poorly handled facilitation, or by circumstances outside the conversational space that may be overwhelming for some conversants. In healthy conversation, participants are able to express their emotions in ways that are helpful to the conversation. One specific way to healthfully handle emotion is to recognize our defensiveness and the ways it can derail conversations. For facilitators, Schwarz writes, "[Helping] a group deal with emotion means showing group members how to use their emotions and thinking to inform each other, rather than avoid emotions or allow them to control the conversation; it also means helping group members express their emotions positively."[6] Indeed, facilitation can be tricky and often frustrating work, but it is an essential form of leadership in cultivating conversations. A congregation might consider providing training for facilitators (or potential facilitators) on how to navigate the dance of facilitation well.[7]

Cohesive Conversations

A final important facet of improving conversational dynamics in your congregation—especially for medium- to large-sized churches—is the challenge of how to get as many people as possible engaged in the conversation and, at the same time, to do so in a way that builds up the church as a whole rather than splintering it along the lines of smaller conversation groups. This sort of strategy for cohesion must be deeply rooted in the conviction of our call to unity as Christ's body. Ultimately, every church's strategy for cohesion will be unique but will have to address a similar array of questions.

First, how can our conversations be open to all, structured in a way that all members are invited, encouraged, and perhaps even expected to participate? In groups of more than fifty people, it is difficult, if not impossible, for conversation to be open. If your church is committed to having conversation groups of fifty or fewer people, how is the congregation to be sorted into these groups? If the groups are largely homogeneous—as they likely will be if they are sorted by age, life stage, or geography—then it will be much more difficult for the groups to cohere as a single church community. Although it could be more logistically challenging, assigning groups by some random factor (such as the first letter of people's surnames) will be more likely to achieve heterogeneous conversation groups.

Another crucial question, and perhaps a more challenging one, is, How do these conversation groups cohere with one another as the body of Christ? One possible strategy is to have a less frequent but still regular conversation (perhaps quarterly or biannually) with two or three representatives from each conversation group. Having at least two representatives ensures a broader perspective than that offered by a single representative from each group and reduces the likelihood of misrepresentation. This larger conversation may surface disagreements or pressing questions that the church will need to discern. These questions can be directed back to the smaller conversation groups for reflection.

Another possible strategy is to invite all members of the church to topical forums on a particular question. These forums, which could easily be larger than the ideal size for conversation, could be used either as an alternative to the layered representative conversations described above or in addition to layered conversations as a way for the church to wrestle with pressing questions as a whole. A forum, while still a sort of conversation, will need different ground rules to maintain order and openness than those needed for a smaller conversation group. These ground rules could include, for example, a time limit on how long one person may speak and a process for hearing a variety of perspectives and deciding how the church ought to move forward on the basis of these perspectives.

The aim of conversation is not necessarily to make decisions about how the church will act, and conversation should not be seen as an alternative or a threat to existing polity and decision-making structures. Rather, conversations should be seen as a means to discern how the Holy Spirit is moving amid our body as a whole and therefore something to which the congregation's decision makers should seriously and prayerfully pay attention. As I stated in chapter 1, conversation is a means to presence, to learning how to live together as a single body in which no member is taken for granted, in which the gifts God has provided in each member can be put to use, and in which the pains that each member feels can be taken seriously and the burden of these pains can be shared by other members.

Resistance to Conversation

One important aspect of conversational dynamics that cannot be ignored, however awkward or painful it might be, is the question of how we respond to the resistance that some of our members might have to the practice of conversation. Resistance as I refer to it here is not the hesitancy of a shy or introverted person to speak up in a conversation but rather the obstinacy of those who do not want to show up for conversation and who sometimes may inhibit others from participating as well. Any reflection on this kind of resistance should begin with the realization that as much as we desire all members of our congregation to participate in our conversations, we will likely have some members who just won't participate, and we will do more harm than good in trying to force their participation. Resistance to conversation calls for the pastoral work of listening, specifically listening to why these members are resistant to conversation.

To say that this is pastoral work does not mean that it can or should be done solely by someone on the church's pastoral staff.

Any church leader with the gifts of patience, listening, and compassion can enter into this work. The resistance might be logistical, an opposition to when and where the conversation is taking place. Logistical concerns can be addressed in time, but they may simply be a cover for deeper sorts of resistance. Unfamiliarity might be another form of resistance. Ultimately, concerns about unfamiliarity should be met with gentle encouragement to at least try conversation, even if initially only as an observer.

Some of the deepest hostility, however, may come from those who don't really *want* to participate in the life of the church. They want to consume the apparent religious benefits of belonging to a church but have distinct boundaries in their minds about how far they are willing to go in their participation. A first line of response to this kind of resistance is the gentle insistence that our church is a body in which all members need to participate together in order for the body to be healthy and mature. Stating this conviction will probably not change the minds of many resisters, but it is to everyone's benefit to be clear on the nature of the church community.

Beyond emphasizing this conviction, we find a spectrum of other possible responses to this kind of resistance: at one end of the spectrum, a hands-off approach that recognizes their resistance and at the same time welcomes them to continue journeying with the church in hopes that their hearts will eventually be changed, and at the opposite end of the spectrum, a response that lovingly encourages them, and perhaps even works with them, to find another church that is more suited to passive membership. The pastoral responses of church leaders may land all over this spectrum in their efforts to lovingly and gracefully minister to members who are resistant to conversation.

In many churches, the initial resistance to conversation may likely be widespread. A first response to this resistance could be firm but gentle scriptural teaching on our calling to be Christ's body and on the virtues of conversation for helping us cultivate the fruit of the Spirit: "love, joy, peace, patience, kindness, generosity, faithfulness, gentleness, and self-control" (Gal. 5:22–23). Beyond emphatic teaching on conversation, many congregations in which resistance is widespread might need to begin with a conversation on functioning together as a single body and the importance of conversation to that effort. An initial conversation of this sort creates a space in which resistance can openly—and hopefully safely—be named and explored. Although it may never be understood by some resistant members, one of the greatest and most winsome virtues of conversation is that it embraces resistance— allowing it to be spoken and discerned as part of the way forward, rather than simply stifling it.

In terms of understanding and responding to resistance, we would do well to remember our calling to function together as a body. Like many of the anatomical parts in a human baby, many of our church members don't even realize that we are intimately connected to one another as Christ's body in this place. Culturally, we are accustomed to functioning as individuals, but body parts do not function well apart from the body. Our legs cannot walk very far without the rest of our body energizing and guiding them. A stomach is useless without the mouth, throat, and esophagus to feed it and without the whole body for it to supply energy to.

Another significant cultural problem that feeds resistance to conversation is our hypermobility. Our church bodies are regularly losing body parts and having others transplanted among us. This give and take of body parts is not only painful but it also requires a long time to heal and for members transplanted into our body to adapt and begin working well with the whole body. A certain degree of resistance is to be expected with a new transplant. A person whose body is receiving a transplanted organ takes anti-rejection drugs to help acclimate the new organ to the body. In an analogous fashion, an intentional effort to get to know new people in our congregation—in ways that aren't programmatic or overbearing—will go a long way toward their integration as healthy, functioning members of our body. Simple, genuine conversations over a meal or coffee or dessert are perhaps the most effective way to introduce new people to the conversational life of a church body; these kinds of informal conversations break down barriers that keep new folks resistant to conversation or passive within it.

We can never fully engineer good, healthy conversation, and, indeed, rigid engineering often produces backlash against it. Our attentiveness to the dynamics described in this chapter and how they play out in our particular congregation can help us to cultivate spaces in which transformative conversations can unfold. Formal teaching that emphasizes our call to embody Christ together as a congregation is important but insufficient on its own. Congregation members also need to participate in healthy conversational spaces that invite open, Christlike conversation in which we can continually discover and grow into our deep connections to one another. In these spaces we can learn what Paul meant when he explained that by "speaking the truth in love, we must grow up in every way into him who is the head, into Christ, from whom the whole body, joined and knit together by every ligament with which it is equipped, as each part is working properly, promotes the body's growth in building itself up in love" (Eph. 4:15–16).

3

What Will We Talk About?

Real change begins with the simple act of people talking about what they care about.

—Margaret Wheatley, *Turning to One Another*

Our bodies are always in motion, moving forward second by second through time and space. Even when we sit still as a statue, air is breathed in and out of our lungs; blood flows to our extremities and back; chemicals in our stomach and digestive system are turning food into energy; muscles and bones resist the force of gravity to hold our body still. All of these motions are made possible and coordinated by the intricate conversation of our body parts. The internal conversation between all the members of our body is never merely idle chatter. My liver and lungs are not sitting and chatting about the latest football game or the latest viral sensation on the internet. My eye and my elbow are not engaging in abstract theorizing or speculation. Rather, all parts of my body are talking about their work and mission as members of this particular body, responding to external objects and forces, making split-second decisions, managing a budget of the resources—air, food, or water, for instance—needed to carry on this work, and struggling to adapt when one or more of these resources become scarce.

As we begin to practice conversation in our churches, a crucial question arises: What do we talk about? As we wrestle with this question, we should be ever mindful of the witness of our physical bodies. Just as our bodies are always in motion, our conversations as churches should revolve around the dynamics and activity of our life together as Christ's body in this particular place. How can *all* members—stronger and weaker, more mature and less mature—work together to embody Christ and strive to act together as Christ would act among our particular neighbors? Even when we take seriously our identity as Christ's body and our calling to act together as Christ would act, we face the challenge of deciding among many good and important things that we could talk about. How then do we decide what we should talk about at any given time?

We are always faced with a vast array of possible topics of conversation, but we don't have to be anxious as we decide what to talk about. Our primary goal is learning to embody the mutual presence that characterizes the Trinity, so *how* we talk together is more important than *what* we talk about. While some conversations may be more helpful than others in building up our body, there are no wrong conversations, and we can always move on if we find that a specific conversation is not moving us in the direction of being a healthy embodiment of Christ. In this chapter, we will explore the dynamics of how we discern what we should talk about in our congregational conversations, especially in the earliest stages of our learning to talk together.

What *Not* to Talk About

As a congregation begins to talk together, two types of conversations are decidedly unhelpful: abstract matters and highly charged topics. A time will come when we will indeed need to talk about both of these things, but neither is an especially fruitful place to begin a practice of conversation. Our call is to be a body, a tangible presence of Christ in our particular place, and our conversations should be moving us ever deeper into this calling. To focus too heavily on abstract ideas is to resist the particularity of our calling as God's incarnational people. Theories, general and abstract accounts of how the world works, will inevitably play a role in our conversation, and as they do, it will be helpful to name them. But theories—whether theological, philosophical, psychological, or economic—are most helpful when joined with reflection on concrete situations and on how we understand and function within these concrete realities.

Diving too early or too deeply into abstract theories may be satisfying for a few intellectual types in our congregations who relish thinking and talking about such things, but it will likely lose the interest of the majority of our members. Our churches are concrete social bodies, and while theory can help us understand who we are, where we are, and when we are, it needs to be tightly bound to our existence together as a body. A baby isn't born with the capability for language and abstract thought. Rather, she is concerned solely with concrete actions like eating, breathing, sleeping, and pooping. Learning words and abstract ideas, like mathematics and social theories, are functions of more mature bodies that will develop in due time. Similarly, our churches' conversations should begin with talking about the concrete actions we take together as a body.

The other category we should try to avoid as we are beginning to talk together is highly charged and divisive topics. Our conversation will certainly need to enfold these sorts of questions in due time, but we would do best not to start with them and instead develop trust with one another and some ability to talk together before we attempt to wrestle with such divisive questions. A baby is not born with the capability to walk, let alone walk a tightrope. Similarly, we need to develop some skill, grace, trust, and maturity before we expect to walk the tightrope of highly charged questions without repeatedly tumbling and endangering the life of our body.

Sometimes, however, for the health and well-being of our body, we are forced to dive into such a conversation. Such volatile conversations will be painful, and wounds will surely be inflicted. But if by God's grace our church body survives a conversation of this sort mostly intact, we will learn much about conversation and mature rapidly in the process. Such growth will come at a price, often the loss of some members. Before you leap into a highly charged conversation, consider the cost.

Here at Englewood Christian Church, we made this mistake. One of our earliest conversations wrestled with the question, What is the gospel? As an evangelical church at the time (we are probably more conflicted about that identity today than we were twenty years ago), this question cut to the very heart of our identity, and many of our members had intensely held convictions about how this question should be answered. Our immaturity in talking together, combined with this charged topic, made our conversations brutal. Some people left the church; others permanently dropped out of our Sunday night conversations. Even those who stayed were pummeled and often wounded by one another's words. In retrospect, we would have done well to start with less contentious questions, and we are proof that although tackling charged questions too early isn't always fatal to the conversation, it's not a course we would recommend to others.

What Then Do We Talk About?

So if we steer clear of abstract questions and highly charged topics, what sorts of topics are better suited to guide us toward healthy habits of talking together? In the previous chapter, I mentioned in passing that one of our first conversations might need to be about *why* we should talk together, thus creating a space for listening carefully to those who are hesitant, confused, or resistant to the idea of conversation. Even in the face of opposition to the practice of dialogue, we model conversation by allowing that opposition to be named and explored. The nature of conversation is fundamentally about listening and being present with others in our community as we learn to practice the sort of mutual presence that is inherent in the Trinity. To have a conversation about why we are resistant to conversation can serve to create trust that voices of opposition will be heard and prayerfully considered as a vital part of our dialogue. A conversation of this sort might be most effective when combined with teaching (e.g., a sermon series or a class) on the virtues of learning to talk together. Teaching will provide the framework of a rationale for talking together that can be tested and explored in conversation. Talking about the resistance to conversation that some people in the congregation may have could open the door to exploring deeper questions about authority, divine action and human action, or the nature of our life together, for example. These deeper questions will lay the foundation for future conversations.

Discerning Ground Rules

Another conversation that we should have in the earliest stages of our learning to talk together has to do with establishing ground rules for *how* we desire to talk together. Every community should have its own set of ground rules for conversation, even if these agreements remain unwritten. It can be helpful to start by reading and discussing ground rules that other churches have established for themselves. (A few examples are included in appendix A at the end of this book.)

Ground rules make explicit our intention to embody the love and compassion of Christ in our conversations. They offer specific ways our particular community commits to doing this as we talk together. For example, here are a few of the agreements that Silverton Friends Church (in Silverton, Oregon) makes as they have conversations together:

> We will embody the fruit of the Spirit: love, joy, peace, patience, kindness, goodness, faithfulness, gentleness, and self-control.
> We will acknowledge Christ's presence among us and in each one of us.
> We will look for opportunities to find common ground.
> We will not be afraid of silence.

Ground rules should be selected with care and should be clearly worded so that all members of the body who participate in our conversations can agree to them. Any concerns about a proposed ground rule need to be heard and reflected on. If a resolution that is agreeable to all cannot be reached, it is best to omit this proposed rule.

Our set of ground rules should be a dynamic list that we regularly (but not *too* often) revisit and revise as needed. We also will need practices of introducing these ground rules to new members and of reaffirming our commitment to them. Particular experiences in our conversations may highlight the need to add or remove ground rules.

Ground rules are a crucial aspect of good facilitation. One part of a facilitator's role in helping to keep a conversation on track is ensuring that the group adheres to the ground rules it has established. If the facilitator perceives what seems to be a violation of the ground rules, he or she should pause the conversation and gently inquire with the apparent offender about whether that person has breached the group's ground rules. The aim of addressing apparent violations of ground rules should always be the sustaining of good, healthy, Christlike conversation, not the shaming or punishment of offenders. Even when we have an unresolvable disagreement about whether a ground rule was breached in a certain instance, we demonstrate our commitment to these ground rules and to allowing them to give shape to our conversations.

A Guide for Conversation

As your church is beginning to talk together, you might feel like you need a guide of some sort, something to help direct your conversations and lead you into a deeper understanding of why and how churches should talk together. One resource that was helpful for our church, and has likewise been fruitful for other congregations, is a set of materials from the Congregational Formation Initiative (CFI). Compiled by the Ekklesia Project, an ecumenical group whose mission is to cultivate healthy local church communities, the CFI resources aim "to help initiate and sustain congregational conversations about the fundamental identity and mission of the church."[1]

The first segment of the CFI process consists of two guided conversations, each of which has been published as a workbook. These conversations "begin with the assumption that the church in our day needs to think carefully and discuss openly what it means to be the church. Just as it's difficult to imagine that a business, school, or athletic team could accomplish its purpose if participants had very different and possibly competing understandings of what that purpose was, so it is with the church. If the church gathers each week with vastly different and competing understandings of what it means to be the church, it's hard to imagine that things will go well."[2] The first book, *The Shape of Our Lives*, consists of seven conversations that explore the ways we are formed and malformed by our choices and by the structures of life that surround us. After an initial conversation on formation, the subsequent conversations explore desires, convictions, character, stories, practices, and institutions.

The second book, *The Shape of God's Reign*, is built on a series of three questions:

> What do we think the purpose of church is, and where do our notions about this come from?
>
> Is it possible that our host culture has shaped us to think about the church in ways that are unhelpful, if not unfaithful?
>
> What is God doing in the world, and how have we as the church been called to participate with God in that work?[3]

After three introductory conversations that set the stage, four concluding conversations explore characteristics of the shape of God's reign: wholeness, truthfulness, forgiveness, and reconciliation.

Beyond these two initial series of conversations, CFI provides several discussion guides for important theological books, including Dietrich Bonhoeffer's *Life Together* and Lesslie Newbigin's *Mission in Christ's Way*. If your initial conversations seem a bit unsteady and you want some resources to guide your early conversations, the CFI materials are an excellent place to start.

Discussing Sermons

Another helpful topic for congregational conversations is discussion of the sermons that are preached in the church. This sort of conversation works especially well if your church gathers weekly for conversation, but even if you gather less frequently, it is still possible—and can be fruitful—to discuss sermons. Conversations about sermons can be flexible and could be used as a default when there is not a more urgent topic of conversation. Sermon conversations, when done carefully, can help integrate the church's life together with the scriptural story and create a space where a more broadly shared interpretation of the biblical text, and not simply the preacher's interpretation, can emerge. The common life of most churches contains precious few spaces in which the meaning of Scripture is wrestled with and talked about. Reflecting together on a sermon can be a natural step into the work of understanding and interpreting Scripture together.

In order to spur conversation about a particular sermon, a congregation can do several things. First, my experience has been that a conversation about a sermon is most lively when it is *not* facilitated by the person who preached it. To this end, identify a facilitator in advance of when the sermon will be preached. Ask that person to pay close attention during the sermon and to generate a list of at least five questions that come to mind as they listen and reflect. These questions can be inserted into the conversation if it starts to fizzle and participants run out of sermon-related questions for the group to discuss. The conversation will likewise benefit if the congregation is reminded before the sermon—by a liturgist or worship leader, or by the preacher—that the sermon will be discussed in an upcoming conversational meeting; thus congregants are encouraged to jot down questions or other thoughts that cross their minds as they listen to the sermon.

When talking about a sermon, it is helpful to begin the conversation by reading the scriptural text that the sermon explored. Hearing the text may refresh some members' memories and raise additional questions about the sermon or the text itself. The scriptural passage is the primary topic of conversation, and the sermon is merely a particular lens on that passage. Some members, however, may have questions about the text that the sermon didn't address, and such questions should be fair game for the conversation, as long as they are understood to be beneficial to the life and flourishing of the church. (Questions that are antagonistic, highly abstract, or speculative, for instance, will likely be of little benefit to the life of the church.) The conversation will be most beneficial if it stays focused on two primary ends: (1) understanding the scriptural text, especially within the broader story of Scripture and (2) stirring the congregation's imagination for what the passage might mean for the shape of its life together. The practice of reflecting on and talking about sermons, of wrestling with the meaning of particular biblical texts, can lead us into broader conversations about who we are as the body of Christ and what God is up to in our midst.

Identity: Who Are We?

These conversations are crucial to discerning our identity and deepening our understanding of who we are as a church. Our identity is never static, set in stone, but rather changes over time, as our body matures and as the people and the environment around us also change. Consider, for instance, your own personal story. You are not the same person now that you were at age 2 or 7 or 12 or 17 or 22 or 27. Your interests and your goals for yourself have likely made drastic shifts across the years of your life. Your body and your mind can likely do things now that they couldn't do when you were an infant, a toddler, or an adolescent. In contrast, there may also be some activities that you can't do as well as when you were younger. I cannot run as fast or as far, nor can I lift as much weight as I could when I was a teenager. Our human bodies are ever changing, and these changes affect our self-understanding and our identity. Similarly, our churches need regular, ongoing conversation about who we are and what we are about. We should be conscious that a conversation about identity may be highly charged, as some people may see it as an opportunity to wield power in determining the direction of the church. As such, it is likely not a great topic with which to start a practice of conversation, as it will require some degree of grace and skill. But as we mature in our capacity to talk together, a conversation about our identity as a people is one that we cannot escape.

One of the conversational practices that we have here at Englewood Christian Church is to take an annual all-church retreat over Labor Day weekend, which allows us to get away for a few days and to have extended conversations that we might not otherwise have. (We also have a lot of fun relaxing, playing games, and telling stories together.) For one of our retreats almost a decade ago, our pastor compiled a list of questions to get us thinking about our particular identity as a church:

1. According to the Bible, what is the ultimate end to which God is bringing all of creation? What is God doing in and with the world?

2. According to the Bible, how has God chosen to accomplish God's mission in the world? What is the role the church has been given?

3. What are the particular strategic initiatives to which God has called Englewood in participation with God's mission?

4. What is the place of our covenant agreements in Englewood's shared life? How have we used them in the past and how could we use them in the future?

5. What are our current practices for nurturing intentional congregational formation? What should we give more attention to or what should we change?

At this retreat, we bumbled around quite a bit, had more than a few disagreements, and didn't make much progress toward substantial answers to these questions. We found, however, that these questions didn't die off after the retreat. We discussed them for several months afterward in our weekly Sunday evening conversations. During the intervening years, these questions have come to be a touch point to which we occasionally return in our conversations. They have become an avenue for regularly reflecting on our identity together as a church and how that identity is changing as our body matures and changes with time. We will return to conversations about identity in chapter 8, as they are essential to the work of sustaining our practices of talking together.

How Can We Work Better Together?

The more we use our human bodies for particular activities, the more we begin to identify ourselves with these actions. A young person who loves baseball, for instance, will constantly practice catching, throwing, and hitting the ball and will, through this practice and actually playing in baseball games, increasingly identify as a baseball player. A similar thing is true for our churches: our identity is intimately connected with the things we do. This suggests that another fruitful conversation might involve talking about the various sorts of work we do together as a church—from taking care of and teaching children to caring for elderly members to loving and serving our neighbors, and many other examples.

A conversation about a particular area of work could include an update on what is currently being done and some careful reflection on how we might go deeper in this work. Care is needed because some people involved in the work may be especially sensitive and perceive a conversation about how the work can continue to grow and mature as criticism that the work isn't currently being done well. Ideally, those presently doing the work should lead the conversation about their hopes and dreams for that work and what next steps might be taken. Not only are they the ones most familiar with the specifics of the work, but having them lead the conversation can minimize the perception that the work isn't being done well.

A healthy conversation about the work we do together as a church should include frank but loving assessments of what isn't going well or what could be done better. These conversations should be undertaken as a body that is unified in its desire to bear the burden of any shortcomings, not to shame those who are leading and doing the work. When one part of the physical body is tired, sore, or injured, the rest of the body works together to adapt to this challenge. The same should be true for our churches.

Even when the work is going well, we can benefit from reflecting on it and talking about how we can continue to grow deeper in it and do it more faithfully to the way of Jesus. Reading can help us kick-start conversations in which we reflect on a particular part of the work we do.[4] For instance, those working with people in poverty might read and discuss *When Helping Hurts*, by Steve Corbett and Brian Fikkert, or simply a portion of it. The passage under discussion doesn't have to be long, but it should challenge readers to think in new ways and to ask significant questions that spur further conversation. Even with little or no reflection on how the work can be done better, the body will benefit from knowing what types of work are being done throughout the church and from knowing the people who are coordinating that work.

Divisive Issues

Although I emphasized at the beginning of this chapter that divisive issues are not an ideal launching point for a practice of conversation, they are something that we should talk about at some point, for the health and well-being of our church body. Too many churches ignore difficult issues for as long as possible, creating elephants in the room that everyone is aware of but cannot address. When we do address conflicts in churches, we often do so in an unhealthy manner, through means other than conversation—executive orders or, in some extreme cases, church splits. If we want to be a unified body, we will have to learn to talk about and work through the issues that threaten to divide us. "Tensions should neither be hidden nor be brought prematurely to a head," writes Jean Vanier. "They should be taken on with a great deal of sensitivity and prayerfulness, trust and hope, knowing that there is bound to be suffering. They should be approached with deep understanding and patience, with neither panic nor naive optimism, but with a realism born of a willingness to listen and a desire for truth even if it is challenging and it hurts."[5]

Silverton Friends Church in Oregon, introduced earlier in this chapter, began having intentional conversations about five years ago. These conversations began in a forum class, a common venue in the Friends tradition for listening to one another and talking about pressing social issues. This class assembled a list of agreements that defined how they would talk with one another. The conversations covered topics that ranged from health and nutrition to guns, immigration, and the American dream. These conversations often took unexpected turns. "People who disagreed with us," one member recalled, "often surprised us." These forum conversations about social issues later morphed into Soup Night conversations on Sunday nights, where members shared a simple meal of soup and talked about various facets of life together in their church. Often the conversations involved a discussion of a recent sermon.

After continuing in these conversations for several years, it became apparent that there was an elephant in the room that most members were not yet ready to talk about—namely, how their church should relate to people in the LGBTQ community. At the time, their denomination, the Evangelical Friends Church, was being torn apart over questions related to human sexuality. Since the church already had some experience in the practice of conversation, one member proposed they spend the better part of a year reading a number of books by evangelicals with varying perspectives on sexuality. The books were selected, wrote one of the organizers, because their authors are "people who are passionate about following Jesus and who take Scripture seriously, though they often arrive at different conclusions. . . . The object of our time together is not to debate, defend, convince, or mock; it is to create a safe space where we can thoughtfully engage with the texts and with each other with curiosity, compassion, and grace."[6]

Because their church had been learning to talk together over several years, these conversations were relatively civil. The aim in reading and discussing these books was not to make a particular decision about the church's stance on sexuality, although the church did end up clarifying its theological position several years later. The purpose of the book club conversations was to help the congregation think about many of the related issues and to get people of different perspectives listening and talking to one another.

When our church bodies are divided on a particular question, we will not be able to act in a unified and mature way on matters related to that question. As we learn to talk with one another about this particular question, speaking honestly and listening compassionately, we will begin not only developing the capacity to act faithfully in regard to this question but also maturing in our ability to talk about other questions that divide us.

Our churches have no shortage of things that we could talk about. Indeed, to borrow a thought from the apostle Paul, everything is permissible, but not everything is beneficial (1 Cor. 10:23). The challenge is to find a question or topic that is relevant to the church's present situation, and one that the body is mature enough and ready to discuss. In choosing a topic of conversation, we shouldn't be anxious about whether we are mature enough to talk about a particular question. Either there will be a clear consensus that we aren't ready to talk about it, or, if there is not, we probably are safe to start a conversation on that question. We may bumble around a little (or even a lot) in our conversations, but that bumbling is an opportunity for us to learn how to talk together—extending patience, and perhaps even forgiveness, to one another. We may talk about a question for a season, then realize that we have gone as far as we can and decide to shelve the question for a time with the intent of returning to it later. Conversation, we recall, is fundamentally about presence, not about resolving questions. If we get to the point where going any further will incite some portion of our body to respond in a fashion that doesn't reflect the love and compassion of Christ, then we should pause and consider moving on to a different topic of conversation.

In addition to choosing *what* we talk about, we also need to reflect on *how* we want to talk together about a particular question, which is the topic of the next chapter. Different ways of approaching a question can lead us in different directions, sometimes opening us up for more conversation and, at other times, shutting us off to further conversation.

4

The Healing Potential
of Conversational Methods

Scaffolding is only a tool . . . but at times it can be indispensable.
[It] isn't the focus of the construction process; it's simply a tool
to aid in the necessary work.

   —Philip Kenneson et al., *The Shape of God's Reign*

A s a young child, I loved to be active, whether I was out-
doors enjoying nature, playing sports, or just being a
typical kid. Along the way I took my share of tumbles
and often had cuts or bruises to show for it. I once fell on a broken
bottle at a church softball game and ended up with a large bloody
gash on my knee, a severe cut that required four stitches. These
stitches, of course, were not a part of my body, but they were a tool
that helped my body—and, in particular, the skin and flesh on my
knee—to do what it needed to do in order to heal and be well. A
cast on a broken bone functions in a similar way (we will return
to this image of a cast in chap. 9 when we talk about managing
conflicts in conversation). A person with one limb longer than the

other, whether by birth or after an injury, may be required to go through a process of limb lengthening. Historically, this process has involved placing a scaffold outside the limb. The scaffold is attached to wires or pins that go through the skin and are connected to the bone. The bone is then cut in a strategic place, and as this cut heals, the scaffolding is very gradually extended (typically no more than one millimeter per day) in order to lengthen the bone. Newer technologies can do a similar lengthening process with scaffolding that is inserted inside the body and moved using magnets.

Whether stitches, casts, or scaffolding for lengthening bones, external structures are sometimes needed to help our bodies heal or grow in a way that fosters the well-being of the whole body. While these structures may be essential in certain circumstances, they are external to the body, and the aim is usually for them to be removed from the body when they are no longer necessary. A fully healthy body will not need to rely on these kinds of external structures.

In a similar manner, conversational techniques are a kind of scaffolding that bring us together and encourage us to have certain kinds of conversations together, ones that might not be possible without such techniques. They are good and often helpful, but techniques are merely tools that help us learn the art of talking together and are not the most important thing. It is probably not healthy for us to become dependent on a particular conversational method, using it for most of the conversations that we have together, just as it would not be healthy for someone to continue wearing a cast long after the fractured bone has healed.

In this chapter, I will briefly highlight three conversational techniques—Open Space Technology, Appreciative Inquiry, and World Café—exploring how each of them works and the types of conversations that each is well suited to nurture. Like tools in a toolbox, each technique has a certain type of conversation that it is designed to facilitate. Just as we would not try to loosen a screw with a hammer or drive a nail with a pair of pliers, we should use each technique appropriately for the conversation we hope to have together as a community.

Open Space Technology

Open Space Technology (OST) is a conversational method that we at Englewood Christian Church have found helpful. All that is required for this technique is a question to be explored and a group of people to explore it. OST originated in 1985 at the third annual International Symposium on Organizational Transformation. The first two iterations of this symposium were held in a typical conference format, with speakers and panels that were determined in advance. "The consensus of participants [at the first two symposia]," writes Harrison Owen, a leading advocate for OST, "was that the real excitement came in the coffee breaks." They wanted to host a different kind of conference and a different kind of conversation. Owen recalls that "at the point of arrival, the participants knew only when things would start, when it would conclude, and generally what the theme might be. There was no agenda, no planning committee, no management committee, and the only facilitator in evidence essentially disappeared after several hours. Just 85 people sitting in a circle. Much to the amazement of everybody, 2 ½ hours later we had a three-day agenda totally planned out including multiple workshops, all with conveners, times, places and participants."[1]

The method of OST follows the pattern of this initial gathering. No detailed agenda is brought to the meeting, only a single question or topic. In my experience, OST is most helpful when the topic is broad and the community is working to understand it and to organize themselves in relation to it. An OST conversation begins with the opening circle in which all participants are gathered together and the topic of conversation is introduced. In this opening gathering, the group comes up with issues or questions related to the topic they've gathered to discuss. These issues or questions are recorded, as they will provide the shape of the ensuing conversations. Once the group has identified what seem to be the most important issues, a facilitator will remind the group how the process of OST conversation works.

The process of OST is rooted in four principles and one law, which most groups that utilize OST find helpful to name aloud at the outset of their conversation, as a way of introducing this method. The four principles are:

1. *"Whoever comes is the right people."*

   We don't have to wring our hands about who isn't in the room or marginalize some people who have shown up. Everyone has something to contribute to the conversation.

2. *"Whenever it starts is the right time."*

   What matters most is the question being discussed, not the time frame.

3. *"Whatever happens is the only thing that could have"* (be prepared to be surprised).

   Just as we shouldn't be anxious about who is in the room, we also shouldn't be anxious about how the conversation will unfold. Our frustration about its direction is often destructive to the progress of the group.

4. *"When it's over, it's over."*

   We shouldn't feel compelled to extend a conversation just to fill an allotted amount of time. When a conversation is done, we should move on to a different topic.[2]

And the one law—the law of two feet, as described by Harrison Owen—is this: "If at any time [during our time together] you find yourself in any situation where you are neither learning nor contributing, use your two feet and move to some more productive place."[3]

After the facilitator highlights these principles and one law, the group splits into smaller groups—ideally within the same big room—with each group focused on an issue that was raised in the opening conversation. A key expectation of OST is that anyone who identifies an issue in the opening circle should be willing to initiate a smaller group conversation about that issue. These conversations unfold according to the four principles and the law of two feet. Some groups will discuss their issue, reach an end point, and then dissolve, often with their members moving on to other groups. Also, the law of two feet means that some people will eventually choose to move to a different group. Occasionally it will happen that a person who has offered to start a breakout conversation group on an issue will be the only person who shows up to talk about that issue. In this case, the person might take the time to write down a few of their thoughts on the issue, or they may simply move to another small group conversation. Each small group decides how it will talk about its designated issue, identifying facets and subquestions that need to be discussed. When a predetermined amount of time has passed, all the small groups reconvene in the large group for the closing circle. In this concluding time, the small groups may briefly recap the crucial parts of their conversations, and then the large group decides its next steps on the basis of what has emerged over the course of all the conversations. Pressing questions that are typically addressed include: What do we most need to talk about? How and when are we going to have these continuing conversations?

One particularly memorable experience of utilizing OST here at Englewood Christian Church was our 2005 annual retreat, which was held on Labor Day weekend, mere days after Hurricane Katrina had ravaged New Orleans. It was widely expected that Indiana would see a wave of people migrating north to escape the hurricane's destruction. Faced with the prospect of extending hospitality to these migrants, we wanted to explore specifically what we could do as a church. The immediacy of reacting to the hurricane didn't allow us to get a plan or agenda in place before our retreat. Rather, we gathered with this question on our minds, and we brainstormed various possible scenarios that might unfold over the next few weeks—from a massive influx of migrants who could be housed briefly in our fellowship hall to a handful of families who could stay temporarily in some of our homes.

We also discussed how we could all engage in this work of emergency hospitality, from cooking meals to providing clothes, toiletries, or other necessary items to hosting guests in our homes. From this brainstorming session we divided into groups that focused on particular aspects of the work we identified (e.g., food, transportation, or housing), and each of us at the retreat chose an area in which we thought we could contribute to the conversation and eventually to the work that would need to be done. We had these breakout conversations, and then gathered the whole group together again. Each group summarized its conversation, and slowly a plan emerged for how we would respond.

OST works well when we are faced with a new question or issue that we haven't thought much about. It provides a structure that helps us work together as a body to give some shape to the question at hand and how we will begin to think about it. OST can help us map out a series of conversations that we will need to have around a particular question. The ensuing series of conversations is not likely to proceed in the OST fashion, but OST can help us to discern the most pressing issues we need to discuss and then to launch these conversations. One of the greatest virtues of OST is precisely its openness, which challenges us to approach the particular question as a whole body, all members having a say and encouraged to speak about and explore facets of the question about which they are most passionate.

OST is not as helpful when the conversation is less open, when leaders or some other sector of the large group bring an agenda that they intend for the whole group to adopt. Noted OST facilitator Michael Herman has observed that this process does not work well when

> leaders believe they already know the answer(s) and are looking for ways to sell or impose those ideas on the rest of the organization;
>
> leaders believe that they are the only ones responsible for, or really necessary for, the organization to do its best work;
>
> leaders are seeking the appearance of participation but are unwilling or unable to deal openly and directly with high passion or concern, increasing complexity, real diversity of people or opinions, and/or the urgent need to make decisions and take action.[4]

OST is also not as helpful for churches or groups that need to discern a very specific question on a tight timeline because it tends to open up questions more than to move toward a specific decision.

Appreciative Inquiry

Another conversational technique that can be helpful for giving shape to certain conversations is Appreciative Inquiry (AI). Developed at Case Western Reserve University, AI took shape in reaction to an overreliance on problem solving, which has the tendency to obsess about problems and shortcomings instead of acknowledging the real signs of an organization's growth and progress. AI is

> the cooperative, coevolutionary search for the best in people, their organizations, and the world around them. It involves systemic discovery of what gives life to an organization or a community when it is most effective and most capable in economic, ecological, and human terms.
>
> In AI, intervention gives way to inquiry, imagination, and innovation. Instead of negation, criticism, and spiraling diagnosis,

there is discovery, dream, and design; AI involves the art and practice of asking unconditionally positive questions that strengthen a system's capacity to apprehend, anticipate, and heighten positive potential. Through mass mobilized inquiry, hundreds and even thousands of people can be involved in cocreating their collective future.[5]

AI is especially helpful for churches and groups that need to establish a vision for how they will move forward into the future. Your church may be doing significant things, but if you do not have a vision for why you are doing them and for the direction you believe God is calling you, then AI can provide a structure for conversations to discern together the direction of God's leading.

Although AI allows for some flexibility, it is composed of five basic processes:

1. Choose the positive as the focus of inquiry.
2. Inquire into stories of life-giving forces.
3. Locate themes that appear in the stories and select topics for further inquiry.
4. Create shared images for a preferred future.
5. Find innovative ways to create the future.[6]

These basic processes guide us in the direction of a plan for our future that is rooted in the best parts of our past. Specifically, we begin with our commitment to focus on the positive parts of our history. Although there are many failures and broken parts of our past, we exercise gratitude by focusing on the very best stories from our life together. This focus on the positive will be reinforced in the AI process by the facilitators who lead these conversations. This commitment to exercise gratitude and to focus on the best stories sets the tone for the entire AI process. After setting the tone, the group reflects together on stories in which the congregation in whole or in part was energized or infused with life. Facilitators may probe these stories by asking questions and trying to flesh them out in as much detail as the memory of the group will allow: Who was involved? What exactly happened? What were the fruits of this action? Encouraging diverse members to recount a particular story will help to enrich the collective memory of what unfolded.

As the body of life-giving stories expands, the group should pay attention to common themes that emerge in many of these stories. Focusing on these themes may elicit more stories that follow in a similar vein. The group hears the stories that have been collected and listens to them with an ear for commonalities that weave their way through many or all of them. This search for themes among our stories is a means of interpreting what God has been up to in the midst of our congregation. "By locating these themes," writes Mark Lau Branson in *Memories, Hopes, and Conversations*, his very helpful book on AI, "this interpretative process, which may continue to encourage additional stories, forms basic directions for the church's future."[7]

In the next phase of the interpretative process, the congregation picks one or more of the most significant themes and imagines how these themes might continue to unfold in the future. This step requires significant imagination, painting a picture in our minds of what it might look like for a particular life-giving theme to be carried into the future. The final step of the AI process involves developing an innovative strategy for how the key themes might be acted on as we move into the future. Prior to this final step of the process, we have developed a vision, and we conclude the process by talking about the specific structures and objectives we will need in order to live out the vision we have discerned. Branson notes that these plans for moving forward may be formal or informal. Informal plans could include personal practices to which church members commit themselves or practices that are undertaken in pairs or in small groups (e.g., visiting the sick or studying

Scripture). Formal plans would be ones that unfold within the polity of a given congregation—the action of a committee or the formation of a new committee.[8]

Branson tells the story of how his California church, First Presbyterian Church Altadena, used AI to structure conversations about its future. Faced with the recent departure of a pastor and the reality of declining membership, the congregation decided to take on an AI conversation in order to begin forming a vision for their future. This conversation was led by the church's Mission Assessment Committee. This committee was intrigued by AI's positive emphasis. Although the church would eventually need to call a new pastor, it chose to focus more broadly on exploring its identity in its life and ministry together. With the AI process in mind, the committee assembled a list of questions about the church's past and present that it would ask members of the congregation:

1. Reflecting on your entire experience at First Presbyterian Church Altadena, remember a time when you felt the most engaged, alive, and motivated. Who was involved? What did you do? How did it feel? What happened?

2a. What are the most important contributions the church has made to your life? Tell me when this happened. Who made a difference? How did it affect you?

2b. Don't be humble; this is important information: What are the most valuable ways you contribute to our church—your personality, your perspectives, your skills, your activities, your character? Give some examples.

2c. When have you known the most significant spiritual growth for yourself and the church? When were you growing as a disciple? Think about lessons regarding beliefs or steps of faith. Tell me how this has happened. What made a difference? Who was most helpful?

3. What are the essential characteristics or ways of life that make our church unique?
4. Make three wishes for the future of our church. Describe what the church would look like as these wishes come true.[9]

After compiling these questions, the committee made a plan for the interviews. Time didn't allow for every member of the congregation to be interviewed. The committee had already been studying the demographics of the congregation and named seven distinct groups that made up the vast majority of the church community. Drawing from these groups, Branson notes that the committee "tried to balance our values for wide participation, variety of perspectives, and a special appreciation for the seniors who were the majority"[10] as they set about selecting whom to interview. The committee then conducted these interviews, taking copious notes that would be used to discern common themes among the members' stories. Although a larger number of themes emerged, the congregation condensed them into five key themes.

The committee took these themes and fleshed them out into specific proposals for moving forward. They took care to word the proposal as if it were already true. For example, this excerpt is from one proposal and responds to an identified theme (namely, the congregation's ethnicity—their distinctively Japanese heritage as well as their present desire to nourish diversity): "We have a special interest in how the stories of our Japanese American members shape our life and mission. We are also seeing how the encounter with the stories, values, and connections of other cultures enriches our life and mission. We celebrate this inter-cultural life—not as a way to diminish the richness of our cultures, but as a way to enjoy and benefit from what we believe to be both a gift and a task from God."[11]

This proposal gave vision and direction to the church, and they began to engage the Japanese American seniors in their congregation. One specific step they took was to begin another

AI conversation that identified three areas in which the congregation could deepen their care for the older Japanese American members of their church: (1) relationships; (2) faith, worship, and Scripture; and (3) matters of daily life, such as finances, housing, and transportation.[12] With these areas in mind, the church began developing specific plans that would guide their work in these three directions. This work is ongoing, but the church's AI conversations set them on a course toward a deeper identity as a community and a deeper connection with one another as members of that body.

AI excels at fostering a very specific kind of conversation. For churches, it can help us reflect on our congregational history and the ways the Spirit has been at work drawing us closer together and leading us deeper into the rich, interdependent life of Christ. It also can help us leverage this history in order to envision a plan for moving forward.

As important as these conversations are, however, they are only one type of conversation. AI is not designed to help us have other types of conversations: wrestling with the meaning of a particular Scripture passage or making discernments about how we should respond in a particular situation, for instance.

World Café

One final conversational method that can be useful for structuring conversations is World Café, a technique developed by Juanita Brown and David Isaacs. World Café emerged in 1995 at a small gathering of prominent business leaders who were exploring the topic of intellectual capital. As the story goes, the group had planned to meet on an outdoor patio but was forced inside by a rainstorm. Isaacs had the idea to set up a number of small tables, which would encourage participants to cluster around them and talk freely. The group was instructed to converse around these tables before converging for conversation with the whole group.

These mini conversations were seeded with a question from the previous day's meeting, and they turned out to generate lively dialogue. Someone had the idea to retain one "host" at each table and have the other participants rotate to a different table, spreading the mini conversations around the room. After another hour or so of conversation, each group picked a different host, who stayed at the table while everyone else rotated again. After several rounds of rotation, the group circled up as a whole. This process, recalled Isaacs, "somehow enabled the group to access a form of collaborative intelligence that grew more potent as both ideas and people traveled from table to table, making new connections and cross-pollinating their diverse insights."[13]

This initial gathering offered the structure for what would become the process of World Café. In short, a "World Café generally consists of three rounds of progressive conversation lasting approximately twenty to thirty minutes each, followed by a dialogue among the whole group."[14] Each table conversation will ideally have four or five participants, and the room should have enough tables to support several conversations of this size. The number and length of the rounds are flexible and can be adapted to fit a particular group and setting. Conversation flows through this basic structure and is guided by seven basic, integrated principles:

1. *Set the context.* Make sure the purpose and the parameters of the conversation are clear so participants know what to expect.

2. *Create hospitable space.* Participants should be comfortable and feel safe to talk about the given topic.

3. *Explore questions that matter.* Come into the conversation with a tight focus on the most important questions the group needs to tackle.

4. *Encourage everyone's participation.* The World Café process works best when *all* participants contribute fully.

5. *Cross-pollinate and connect diverse perspectives.* Look for the ideas that are emerging as diverse participants talk together.

6. *Listen together for patterns, insights, and deeper questions.* Focus on areas of convergence (not divergence) and seek constructive results that move the group forward.

7. *Harvest and share collective discoveries.* In the final whole group conversation, record—in brief text or diagrams—the emerging insights from the conversational process.

Hope Fellowship, a congregation in Texas, was exploring how it would identify itself on questions of sexuality. The church's conversations were leading it in the direction of a "third way"[15] that would emphasize the unity of their body, even amid diverse convictions about sexuality. As this community was moving in this direction, they decided to have a World Café conversation to walk through specific scenarios they might face if they adopted a third-way identity. For example, how would they respond if one of their youth came out as a lesbian? Or how would they respond to new worshipers who were beginning to participate regularly with their congregation and who thought that it was a sin for gay people to act on their same-sex attractions? The World Café format gave them the opportunity to reflect on these scenarios and how they might respond faithfully in them as a congregation committed to a third-way identity. One member of this congregation observed, "Using World Café to discuss difficult issues with a large group has provided a way to collect lots of feedback and input from everyone and for people to feel heard and to listen to each other well. World Café is only one tool that we use for discernment at Hope Fellowship, but it has been an important and essential part of our process."[16]

World Café works well in situations like the story above, where the group must wrestle together with the complexity of real-life scenarios. It also works best when the group has a larger block of time for the conversation—at least ninety minutes and preferably two hours. World Café can also be a fitting conversational method in situations where the group members do not know one another very well, as it spurs talking and helps participants get to know many others in the group. Like OST, it works best in an exploratory mode, when the group doesn't know how it will respond to a certain question or situation.

In contrast, World Café does not work well when outcomes are predetermined and the group (or a vocal segment of it) has already decided what it will do. It also does not work well as a method for organizing an initial conversation on a highly charged, polarizing question. (Although sexuality is often such a charged topic, Hope Fellowship, the church in the above story, used World Café to explore specific scenarios that they might eventually face, and not as an initial conversation to wade into the topic.) World Café also will not work well in a group of fewer than twelve people. A group of less than a dozen participants can explore similar questions but will likely be just as effective in doing so as a single group, rather than breaking into smaller table conversations.

—⌇⌇—

The conversational techniques that I have explored in this chapter—Open Space Technology, Appreciative Inquiry, and World Café—are good, useful structures that can help us have certain types of necessary conversations. The structure they provide can nurture conversations in certain situations that help our church bodies heal and grow. I have only briefly sketched the basic contours of these techniques in this chapter. Churches considering using one of these methods for a particular conversation can find a wealth of resources online or in print (see appendix B). Although these methods will help us have certain kinds of conversations by providing the structure and support we need, they cannot guarantee that our church body will be healthy or capable of healing and growing. A doctor can put a cast on a broken bone, but if the patient's bones are brittle or if the patient is not eating well and getting the nutrients needed for healing, a cast will be useless and the fracture will not heal well. In the next part of this book, we will explore some basic contours of a spirituality that helps nurture conversation among our members and that fosters the healing and growth of our church bodies.

PART 2

A SPIRITUALITY FOR THE JOURNEY

5

Conversation as a
Prayerful Way of Being

Eternal Trinity, Godhead, mystery as deep as the sea, you could give [us] no greater gift than the gift of yourself.

—St. Catherine of Siena, *On Divine Providence*

My family lives in a large, century-old house that is well built but regularly has things that need to be fixed. In recent years, for instance, we have had a broken screen door and a couple of places that leak during heavy rainstorms. We restored the house's original painted wood siding, which has spots that peel and have to be scraped and repainted every few years. The house does not have central air conditioning, so every May I lug our window air conditioners up from the basement, clean them, and install them in four or five rooms.

Although I am not exactly the handiest person around, I regularly get called on to fix problems and to keep up with the basic maintenance of our home. Some problems I can easily fix; other times I am not as successful and end up calling in a more skilled friend or a professional. Regardless, my tool bucket is essential to the work of taking care of our house. This bucket contains various screwdrivers, hammers, drill bits, and wrenches, but one of the tools I use most often is my pair of locking pliers. Whether pulling nails or tightening bolts on our washing machine, these versatile pliers have solved many of the problems our house has dealt me.

As useful as these pliers are, however, they are merely a tool. They are not part of my body or my identity. Sometimes I lose track of them for days or weeks—when someone borrows them, for instance, or when I forget to put them back in my tool bucket. These pliers, like any tool, have distinct limits on what they can do; they are not very effective, for example, for scraping and painting wood siding or reglazing a windowpane.

A tool is a means to get something done. Although some tools, like my locking pliers, are more versatile than others, we pick tools—in home repair, in cooking, in office work—that fit the particular end we want to accomplish. A recurring theme in my adventures in home maintenance is the struggle to find the right tool for a particular job. More than a few home projects have ended poorly because I did not know the best tool to use for that job or did not have access to the right tool and settled for an inferior substitute. A tool is also external to its user. Although I can *do* many things with my fingers, I don't think of them as a tool. Rather, they are part of my body and my identity as a human being.

With these definitions in mind, conversation is not a tool we can pick up when convenient and use to accomplish a particular thing. It might be tempting for our churches to think of conversation in this way, as something we fetch when we need to resolve a conflict or determine a course of action. Learning to talk together will likely help us in these ways, but conversation is much more than a tool; it is more like our fingers or our noses—an integral part of who we are as human *beings*. Although we might slide into habits of not using it, conversation is as essential to human life and flourishing as any part or function of our bodies.

When we are first born, our eyes cannot focus, and as a result we don't see very well, but our eyes are no less a part of who we are. Conversation functions in a similar way. We may not be able to talk very well together, but conversation remains the primary way by which we come to know others and make ourselves available to be known by others. Since Adam gave names to the animals at the beginning of human history (Gen. 2:19–20), conversation has been a fundamental element in establishing culture through naming and structuring human experience. Through sensory interactions, naming, storytelling, and imagination, human conversations are constantly structuring and restructuring the world in which we live.

In this chapter and the two that follow, I sketch the outline of a spirituality that will orient us deeper into this conversational way of being. This spirituality has three dimensions that are intertwined with one another: prayer, abiding, and preparation. When Christians in the twenty-first century talk about spirituality, we often do so in very personalized terms, describing the character and practices that empower an individual to mature in his or her following of Jesus. The spirituality that I sketch here is of a different sort, one that describes the character and shared practices of a community. In these chapters, I encourage us all to take a hard look at who we are as congregations and at what sort of soil our life together provides for the growth of conversation.

Praying Together

Prayer is a specific kind of conversation, an ongoing dialogue between humanity and God. Although we each personally pray to God daily in many ways, my focus here will be on the ways that we pray together as a community, what some have called corporate prayer. Prayer is the means by which we learn to enter the transforming presence of God. Similarly, by learning to be present to God, as we pray together, we are learning to be present to one another. Many churches struggle to imagine what it looks like to be present *both* to God and to one another in prayer. I have been in churches where divisions appear as gaping wounds during times of corporate prayer, as factions of the congregation lift up contradictory prayers that seem more to slap the opposition in the face than to appeal to the loving-kindness of God. Although such meetings are called in the name of prayer, there is very little of the spirit of prayer in them, of humbly entering into the presence of God and the presence of our fellow human beings. In liturgical traditions of prayer, although many of us make a concentrated effort to be present with God and with the host of saints who have gone before us, we can be tempted to become oblivious to the flesh-and-blood presence of our brothers and sisters who surround us and to the ways we enter into these prayers together in the fullness of all our gifts and brokenness.

The conversations we have as churches—whether studying together, discussing finances or other church business, or discerning the Spirit's guidance in some pressing question—will be most beneficial when seen as opportunities for prayer, for presence with God and with one another. To enter our conversations prayerfully is to enter them attentively: striving to pay attention not only to how God is leading us but also to one another in verbal and nonverbal communication, to the content and direction of the conversation, and to the context in which the conversation is unfolding. In the age of the smartphone, the giving or receiving of one's undivided attention is strikingly rare. Attention is such a challenge for us, not only because we are surrounded by technologies that distract us but also because we humans are inevitably selfish beings. We may listen, but we are inclined to do so in a manner that largely serves our own personal interests. We often find ourselves more inclined to think about how we will respond or how we can make the conversation tilt in our favor than to actually hearing what the other person is saying. Real attention is more than this sort of self-oriented listening; to be fully attentive, we must focus our attention on more than simply the words that come out of another's mouth. Attentiveness is, in the words of theologian Philip Kenneson, "a kind of listening that attends not just to words, but to subtle shifts in tone, to facial expressions, to body language, and to what remains unsaid."[1]

Prayer Begins in Silence

If we take our times of conversation as times of prayer, we would do well to start in silence. In a world like ours, drunk with noise, silence is an immense challenge. "The word no longer communicates," writes Henri Nouwen, "no longer fosters communion, no longer creates community, and therefore no longer gives life. The word no longer offers trustworthy ground on which people can meet each other and build society."[2] Silence is a discipline of self-control. In silence we prepare our hearts and minds for conversation, reminding ourselves that the end we are seeking is not that of our personal agendas but an encounter with the very presence of God.

In our age, God often seems frustratingly silent. The Jewish theologian Martin Buber has suggested that God seems silent because our expectations are misoriented. God does not come to us triumphantly in the word of certainty; rather, our theophany— our encounter with God—comes much more humbly, as a light refracted through the brothers and sisters with whom we are gathered. Buber eloquently observes, "We expect a theophany of which we know nothing but the place, and the place is called community. In the public catacombs of this expectation there is no single God's word that can be clearly known and advocated, but the words delivered are clarified for us in our human situation of being turned toward one another. There is no obedience to the coming one without loyalty to his creature. To have experienced this is our way."[3]

In silence, we are prepared for this sort of theophany. Silence teaches us to follow the wisdom of the apostle James, being "quick to listen, slow to speak, and slow to become angry" (James 1:19). By beginning our conversations with a time of silence, we focus ourselves on listening to God, and this listening posture is carried with us as we begin prayerful conversation together. Silence thus helps us transition out of the mind-set of the kingdom of this world that is overrun with words and to enter, for a brief, fleeting time, into God's presence, a space in which our primary mode is not speaking but listening.

The Quaker tradition has a long history of practicing silence in the gatherings of their faith communities. Just as the Eucharist in the Catholic tradition is a practice centered on God's presence in the bread and the cup, silence in the Quaker tradition is also a practice of God's presence with our congregation in the Holy Spirit. "The deep silence of the soul," writes noted Quaker author Brent Bill, "is our Eucharist."[4] Silence teaches us how to be humbly and reverently in the presence of God and in the presence of our sisters and brothers with whom we are knit together in the Spirit.

In *Silence and Witness*, one of the most important books on the Quaker practice of silence, Michael Birkel concisely describes the traditional structure of a Quaker meeting: "Quaker meeting is as simple as it is complex. The community gathers together in a waiting, expectant frame of spirit. Worship is in silence until a participant feels led to share a message with those present. There may be many, few, or no such messages, which the Friends call 'vocal ministry.' The meeting concludes when the person with the responsibility for closing the worship discerns that the time has drawn to an end."[5]

Brent Bill described to me a recent meeting of his Quaker congregation in central Indiana, which has been worshiping together for 160 years. The congregation, which had shrunk in size during recent years, needed to decide whether it would continue to exist or would dissolve. A short list of questions, which Quakers call "queries," was compiled in advance and would guide the meeting as participants prayerfully discerned these questions. For this particular meeting each member was allowed to speak only once, and no one was permitted to rebut another's contribution. The congregation sat in silence for a time, and eventually they began responding to the queries one by one. After everyone had spoken, and a few clarifying questions had been asked, the meeting discerned together that they should indeed continue to meet.

Flowing from these congregational meetings that are deeply rooted in silence, Quaker spirituality is defined by the kind of listening that is honed through the practice of silence. Regardless of what stream of the Christian tradition we call home, our practices of conversation will be richer if we are attentive to the Quaker practice of silence. In silence, we listen for the Spirit's guidance regarding whom God desires us to be. In silence, God trains us to see one another, and our neighbors, as God sees them. As our imaginations are renewed and transformed in this way by regularly practicing silence in the presence of our gathered church community, we begin to embody this renewed imagination in our conversations and actions with our sisters and brothers and with our neighbors.

Drawing on the Quaker tradition of silence and the Ignatian tradition of examen (a way of prayer intended to help us discern God's presence and guidance), Grandview Calvary Baptist Church in Vancouver, British Columbia, has developed their own practices of listening prayer. Grandview uses listening prayer in a variety of their gatherings, but the most significant is its use in the annual congregational meeting. After participants divide into small groups, the members of each group reflect in silence on a specific question that is being discerned. Inspired by the charismatic tradition, they try to leave room for the possibility that God might speak in different ways to different members of their body. Joy Banks, one of Grandview's pastors who leads the congregation in the practice of listening prayer, notes that a question might follow this form: "God, we seek your guidance for us as a community in this matter and we want to take time to listen to you now. As we go forward in this process, what is one way that you would like us to grow deeper into your vision of community? Would you give us an image or a word or a sense that would encourage us in that area?"[6]

Eventually, each member of the group speaks in turn, giving words to the guidance that they discerned from the Spirit in the time of silence. Each group discusses how the Spirit might be speaking to them through what each member has heard. When the groups reconvene as one large group, they share and discern what each group has heard, striving to understand how the collective insights of all the small groups might illuminate a way forward on the question that the church is discerning. Grandview members have used this practice of listening prayer to discern a wide range of questions related to their life together and their engagement with their neighbors.

Silence also has the function of teaching us *how* to speak. It is nearly impossible, as the apostle James reminds us, for us to control our tongues. Despite our best intentions, our words get derailed, becoming weapons to manipulate, shame, or wound one another. Henri Nouwen writes that "words can only create communion and thus new life when they embody the silence from which they emerge. As soon as we begin to take hold of each other by our words, and use words to defend ourselves or offend others, the word no longer speaks of silence. But when the word calls forth the healing and restoring of its own silence, few words are needed: much can be said without much being spoken."[7] The spirit of prayer is the submission of ourselves to the will and the way of God. This submission is highlighted in two of Jesus's most familiar prayers. When his disciples asked him to teach them how to pray, Jesus taught them the prayer often known as the Lord's Prayer, which begins with these words:

Our Father in heaven,
>hallowed be your name.
>Your kingdom come.
>Your will be done,
>>on earth as it is in heaven. (Matt. 6:9–10)

These words are so familiar to us that we often miss their impact. In praying "Your kingdom come," we are praying that our own personal kingdoms and wills be submitted to those of God.

Similarly, in the garden of Gethsemane as Jesus faces his imminent arrest, he prays, "Not my will but yours be done" (Luke 22:42). Beginning our conversations together in silence slows us down and reminds us that we are entering a time of prayer, a time of seeking to know God's presence with us, a time of seeking not our own personal interests and agendas but those of the common good—of our church, our neighborhood, and God's creation as a whole. Silence reminds us that we enter humbly into these conversations; we are not saviors of one another or our neighbors. Indeed, amid the messiness of our broken world, we often find ourselves in a place where we don't know what to say or do. Silence teaches us to listen first, instead of speaking. In this posture of silent listening, we demonstrate that God is present with us and that we trust God to guide us and provide abundantly for the journey on which we are called.

Binding What Has Been Fractured

In the introduction to this book, we examined the deep fragmentation of our age. As we gather for conversation, we come face-to-face with this fragmentation. Even congregations that seem to be largely homogeneous contain within themselves a degree of fragmentation—for instance, the varying perspectives that emerge from differences in gender, age, economic class, and educational background. To enter our conversations prayerfully as churches is to come, in all our personal and social brokenness, before the One who is healing and restoring all things. Like Adam and Eve in the garden of Eden, we are ashamed and would prefer to hide our brokenness. In prayer, we are invited to live in the tension that we have *already* been united in Christ and at the same time have *not yet* fully realized that unity in our midst.

As we talk together and seek God's presence with us, we recognize that although we will have disagreements that threaten to divide us, we will work through these disagreements in love and with patience, as we also recognize that we are united in Christ. God desires to heal the fractures in our body, but this healing will come in God's way, not ours—and it will come according to God's timing. Praying and talking together in a way that acknowledges both our unity and our disagreement is a means by which we learn patience. We are powerfully tempted to resolve this tension by either fleeing and pretending it doesn't exist or by fighting it, manipulating or forcing one another toward the unity we proclaim. Patience is a third way that is neither fighting nor fleeing. Nouwen says that "patience means overcoming the fear of a controversial subject. . . . It means welcoming sincere criticism and evaluating changing conditions. In short, patience is a willingness to be influenced even when this requires giving up control and entering into unknown territory."[8]

In our conversations together, we confess our fragmentation and live patiently in the tension of being both unified and divided. We also, however, live in expectation that God's presence with us will heal our wounds and divisions. One way God begins the work of healing in us is through our human presence with one another. As we are present with one another, and particularly with those who differ substantially from us, we come to see them not as members of some opposing group (Democrats, if we are Republicans; the older generations, if we are young, and so on) but rather as fellow human beings and fellow sisters and brothers in Christ, with whom we share abundant common ground.

Indeed, some of the deepest public struggles of the twenty-first century stem from our inability to see those who are different from us as humans created in the image of God and to abide with them in a prayerful sort of relationship that recognizes God's presence with and among us. Black Lives Matter, for instance, is a movement focused on affirming the humanity of people of color, who have for too long suffered systematic and sometimes deadly oppression because of being seen as less than human.[9] Much of our political discourse over the last decade has been fueled by demonization of the other, another virulent strain of seeing our fellow humans as something less than creatures made in God's image.

As we abide in these prayerful sorts of relationships, even with people beyond those who regularly surround us in our church communities and our neighborhoods, one of the most succulent fruits we cultivate is trust. We may not agree with the other person or group of people, but by learning to abide with them, to devote ourselves to their care, and to attentively listen to their stories, we begin to trust them. And in learning to trust other humans in these prayerful sorts of relationships, we also cultivate trust in God, particularly trust that God is at work in the relationship, healing and reconciling, and trust that God will continue to guide us together in the just, loving, and peaceable way of Jesus. When we begin to take baby steps in the direction of prayerful, conversational relationships of this sort, we discover that our trust in other people and our trust in God multiplies exponentially and that we desire to expand these relationships to more people and deeper trust. This change of perspective unfolds slowly as we come to know the other, learning to patiently abide in the tension of being both united and fragmented.

As we converse prayerfully together, learning to be present with one another, we begin by listening, looking first for the common ground we share and not repeatedly battling over issues that divide us. Although we should be honest about our divisions in prayerfully seeking God's presence with us and about our human presence with one another (not pretending that they do not exist), we find that we share much common ground from which we can begin to work together.

Praying without Ceasing

The way of praying and talking together sketched in this chapter helps us imagine what it might look like for us to follow the apostle Paul's instruction to "pray without ceasing" (1 Thess. 5:17). In this way, our times of conversation together form us to be an attentive and compassionate community amid all the facets of our daily lives. As we strive to pray without ceasing, we recognize that God is ever present with us, and we grow attentive to God's presence with us in the midst of our everyday situations. Prayer in these terms could be imagined as abiding with God's presence, devoting ourselves to the work of responding to God's presence and being attentive to how God is communicating with us. Just as God is Triune, three beings existing as one in an eternal conversation, the divine life that God invites us into is a prayerful conversation—God and humanity whirling around each other, God leading and humans responding and attempting, despite our immaturity and finitude, to follow God's lead. Our most important work as the community of God's people is to discern the direction of God's leading together and then to bear witness to the existence and nature of this dance, inviting others to join with us in following its God-breathed rhythms.

We have been created by God to live this conversational life with God—a life of ceaseless prayer—and with those humans with whom God has surrounded us. Conversation should not be reduced to something fun that we do on occasion, nor is it a tool to get things done. Rather, conversation is at the very heart of our being, as humans created in the image of the Triune God, who exists as a conversational community.

The Psalms, which were originally compiled as the prayer book of the ancient Israelites, guide us into this sort of conversational life with God. For the psalmists, no emotion is off-limits in their talking with God—joy, thanksgiving, fear, rage, confusion, and many more. Although God has created us, and is ever present with us, God desires that we articulate our emotions in prayerful conversation. Our lack of transparency with God is often our way of resisting God's transforming work in our lives.

Transparency is fundamentally connected to trust. Do we trust God? Often we do not. The image of God that many of us have inherited—a God who is vengeful, or a God who is far removed from our struggles, for example—is a God we would have good reason *not* to trust. All the bad theology we have inherited, and all our worst fears about God, will ultimately dissolve as we learn to be present with God. Trust is born of knowledge and not simply knowledge *about* a person but rather knowledge *of* a person, the sort that comes from being in a person's presence and being able to translate their facial expressions and body language, for instance. Certainly, this sort of knowledge is much more complicated in the case of God, who is not present with us moment by moment in bodily form. Jesus, of course, was present in bodily form during his earthly ministry, and the Holy Spirit abides with us in our church communities. We grow in our knowledge of God as we encounter God in the scriptural story and in our lived experience. The former is especially so in the Gospels, which reveal the nature and character of God through Jesus. The latter can be seen especially through the work of the Holy Spirit, who teaches us, guides us, and provides for us.

Through these encounters we find that God, whose very nature is love, does not coerce us; rather, by giving voice to our emotions, desires, and struggles, God-with-us is pleased to meet us in the middle of them, to walk alongside us, listening and gently guiding us as we go. In our brokenness we tend to resist this conversational sort of life. We often cannot bear to speak of the fears and distrust that tend to drive our everyday existence. We need forms and rhythms that give us practice whispering these hard truths about our lives.

For centuries, the psalms have been prayed by God's people, first the Israelites and eventually the church as well. Speaking (or in some cases singing) another human's prayers affords us the opportunity to find ourselves in these psalms, to give voice to emotions that might have otherwise gone unspoken. Rhythms of prayer—whether hourly, daily, or weekly—serve as a structure that reminds us of God's presence with us and of our need to carve out time to be present and in conversation with God.

Expect Change

When we learn to seek God together in prayerful conversation and carry these conversations in our hearts and minds, praying without ceasing as we move through our days, we should expect to be changed. From the garden of Eden to John's Revelation, the scriptural story reminds us throughout that to be in God's presence is to be transformed. For instance, when Moses encountered God in the burning bush, he was skeptical that he was the right person to lead Israel out of Egypt, but the encounter with the presence of God powerfully transformed him. By listening to God's guidance, he led the Israelites out of their slavery in Egypt. Similarly, the apostle Peter, as a good Jew, was convinced that he should not eat the meat of unclean animals; an encounter with God's presence convinced him to honor the hospitality offered him in Cornelius's house and to eat whatever they served him—clean or unclean—and to welcome gentiles into God's family. Encountering God's presence changes us.

In prayerful conversation together, we learn that the most important thing is not the agendas we bring with us (and our intuitive sense that we must vehemently defend these agendas). Rather, the most important thing is learning to abide in the presence of God and of our sisters and brothers. To abide does not mean that we cease to have convictions—even convictions that stand in stark contrast to those of others in our congregations—but rather that our personal convictions must take a back seat to the work of learning to be present. It is these encounters with God's presence, and often God's presence refracted through the people of our congregation, that powerfully transform us. Preferring presence to ideology will lead us into a whirlwind of chaos, a storm for which we can anticipate and prepare. In the next chapter, we explore the dynamics of this whirlwind and how we can remain confident of God's presence with us in the midst of it.

6

Abiding in the
Messiness of Life

The value of our weakness is that it teaches us to wait for God's timing, to overcome evil with love, to respond with gentleness instead of violence.

—Marva Dawn, *Joy in Our Weakness*

In the book of Job, we find one of the longest and most intense conversations recorded in Scripture. A great tragedy has fallen on Job. His children were all killed in a great storm, and all of his animals—which in that nomadic culture meant all his riches—were taken from him by neighboring tribes or by firestorms from the heavens. On top of all these crushing losses, Job is afflicted from head to toe with festering boils. In the wake of these tragedies, Job sits in ashes, using a broken piece of pottery to scrape the sores covering his body.

Three of Job's friends—Eliphaz, Bildad, and Zophar—hear of the calamities that have struck Job, and they journey from their homes to be with him and to "console and comfort him" (Job

2:11). They grieve with their friend, not only weeping but also tearing their clothes and sitting with him in the dust and ashes. In an almost unfathomable display of compassion, the three friends sit with Job in utter silence for seven days and seven nights. The silence is broken by Job, who, like many in grief, cannot escape the question, "Why?"

> Why did I not die at birth,
>> come forth from the womb and expire? (3:11)

> Why is light given to one in misery,
>> and life to the bitter in soul,
> who long for death, but it does not come,
>> and dig for it more than for hidden treasures;
> who rejoice exceedingly,
>> and are glad when they find the grave? (3:20–22)

After listening to Job's grieving, his friends break their silence and begin to respond, one after the other. Eliphaz the Temanite begins gently:

> If one ventures a word with you, will you be offended?
> But who can keep from speaking? (4:2)

The advice of Job's friends becomes less and less helpful as the story progresses. Ultimately, the Lord intervenes, engaging Job in conversation and threatening to unleash fury on Eliphaz, Bildad, and Zophar (42:7–9).

The story of Job is a story of the messiness of life, the messiness of the tragedy that falls on Job, and the messiness of Job's friends. "Messiness," as I use it in this chapter, is not a familiar theological term. It is related to the biblical concept of weakness,[1] but it conjures imagery that is more social than personal and may be more accessible to us amid our twenty-first-century Western culture that is pathologically obsessed with avoiding any appearance of weakness. Messiness is a broad concept that describes the situation in which we find ourselves, including personal and social sin. But it also describes tragedy that senselessly falls on us, as well as the sheer limitations of our human knowledge and experience as finite creatures. These facets of messiness intersect with and amplify each other, creating greater chaos that disorients us and ripples through our networks of relationships. In the story of Job, for instance, he faces the effects of social sin—brutal crimes of murder and plunder executed by the Sabean and Chaldean peoples (Job 1:15–17)—as well as the effects of the personal sin of his friends, such as impatience and lack of compassion, and the tragic effects of a windstorm (v. 19) and a plague of boils (2:7–8).

Despite their ultimate crumbling under the pressure of impatience, Job's friends initially offer instructive responses. They gather with Job and are present with him. They sit in silence with him (for seven days and nights!) and then listen to Job's cries for answers in his grief. Although grief, like that which Job experienced, accentuates the messiness of life, we are confronted by the mess of human life at every turn. When we gather for conversation, we come in weakness, bringing with us our personal messes and the social mess of our immediate and extended families, our places and workplaces, and indeed even the mess of our past and present churches.

We have been formed by the forces of the modern age to want neat and simple solutions. Sociologist George Ritzer, in describing life in the present age in his classic book *The McDonaldization of Society*, notes that our fast culture compels us to favor the virtues of efficiency, predictability, quantifiability, and control.[2] The problem, however, is that as much as we desire these virtues, they are simply not compatible with the messiness of life.

By meticulously controlling various components of a particular system, we can create the illusion of these virtues, but often at a great price to people and realities outside this system. A farmer, for instance, can use pesticides to eliminate the messiness of weeds in his soybean fields, but these chemicals may run off his fields into woodlands or rivers, posing threats to land and water creatures and possibly polluting the water supply. A company may start using machines to speed up the production of its widgets and even improve the production quality, but where will the energy to power these machines come from, and at what cost—especially if the energy comes in the form of coal-fired or nuclear electricity? And what will happen to the people whose jobs are replaced by machines? Life is messy, and as we make discernments as churches, we will do well to pay attention as broadly as possible to the ramifications of our decisions.

Rather than trying to force situations and people into our neat categories, we would do better to abide in the messiness of our lives: our own mess, as well as that of others. "Abide" is not a verb that most of us use as a regular part of our vocabulary, and yet it is an important word in the biblical text, one that might be worth recovering in the twenty-first century. Abiding cuts across the grain of late-modern Western culture, with its emphasis on efficiency and productivity. Abiding, writes theologian Philip Kenneson, "is that practice or dimension of presence that involves being with and remaining with another."[3] In perhaps one of the most familiar scriptural uses of this verb, Jesus instructs his disciples in John 15, "Abide in me as I abide in you. Just as the branch cannot bear fruit by itself unless it abides in the vine, neither can you unless you abide in me. I am the vine, you are the branches. Those who abide in me and I in them bear much fruit, because apart from me you can do nothing" (vv. 4–5).

We have been created to abide *in* Christ, who is our Creator and the source of all life. As we abide in Christ, we abide *with* our sisters and brothers in Christ and others, receiving from them the life of Christ. Abiding with another person means remaining in a relationship with a posture that allows one to receive the Christ-given gifts of the other. In a world in which we are quick to part ways with those with whom we have disagreements, abiding is rooted in the hope that the mutual giving and receiving of relationship will be more vital than our disagreements. Abiding is thus an appreciative way to be in relationship that understands the other primarily as a gift, not as a burden or an enemy. Of course, we should not be naive or evasive about problems and disagreements, but through abiding, we commit to learning and sharing together despite the challenges we might encounter along the way.

Abiding is perhaps the primary practice through which we learn the virtue of patience. When faced with difficult situations, our instincts drive us to either fight or flee. Patience is a third-way response that is neither fight nor flight. As Henri Nouwen and coauthors Donald McNeill and Douglas Morrison write in *Compassion: A Reflection on the Christian Life*, patience "calls for discipline because it goes against the grain of our impulses. Patience involves staying with it, living it through, listening carefully to what presents itself to us in the here and now." Abiding is the practice of staying rooted in relationships through difficult seasons because God is teaching us, and providing for us, in the other. As we patiently abide, we "enter our lives with open eyes, ears, and hands."[4] Marriage is perhaps one of the most familiar relationships in which we learn to abide (or if we are not married, we may learn by observing the close, committed relationships of others). The commitment "to have and to hold from this day forward, for better for worse, for richer for poorer, in sickness and in health, to love and to cherish, till death do us part"[5] articulated in marriage vows is a commitment to abide with one's spouse. Similarly, in parenting we learn to abide with our children, even when they are going through adolescence or other particularly difficult seasons.

Amid the hypermobility of life in the twenty-first century, we encounter many forces that make it almost impossible to abide. In this generation it is much easier—when faced with the messiness of life in our workplaces, our churches, and even our homes—simply to cut our ties and move on. The increasing speed of transportation over the last 150 years and the proliferation of communication technologies over the past half century present us with exponentially more opportunities than those offered to our ancestors. These opportunities and choices are not necessarily bad, but they can tempt us to flee when we face difficult times in our present situation. The industrialization of life and the emphasis we place on efficiency and instant gratification also erode our inclination to abide.

As we learn to abide in messiness in the twenty-first century, we would do well to consider our Christian sisters and brothers in the Benedictine tradition, whose vows include a vow of stability, a commitment through thick and thin to a particular faith community. Theologian and Benedictine oblate Gerald Schlabach writes:

> In an obsessively mobile society, one wonders whether Christians can be the body of Christ together at all if we will not slow down and stay longer, even if we cannot stay indefinitely, and practice something like a vow of stability. Slow down: because what many call postmodernism may really be hypermodernism. Stay longer: because there is no way to discern God's will together without commitment to sit long with one another in the first place. A vow of stability: because it is no use discerning appropriate ways to be Christian disciples in our age if we do not embody those ways through time, testing, and the patience with one another that transforms good ideas and intentions into communal practices.[6]

Stability is the commitment in this hypermobile and fractious age to learn what it means to be Christ's body. God's work in creation has been centered around the gathering of a people—from ancient Israel, the descendants of Abraham, Isaac, and Jacob, to Jesus's disciples to the gentiles "grafted in" to the olive tree of Israel (see Rom. 11:13–24). And in every chapter of this story, broken human beings struggle to be the community of God's people together. The story of ancient Israel is full of conflict, even to the point of Israel splitting into two kingdoms. Jesus's disciples quarrel over who will be the greatest in God's kingdom. A sizeable portion of the New Testament Epistles is devoted to helping Jews and gentiles live peaceably together in the church despite their vastly different cultural formations.

The Messiness of Sin

Striving to live in the community of God's people is no less complicated today than it was in the days of ancient Israel or those of the first-century churches. Our calling to follow Jesus is a call to embody Christ with other human beings, and however much we might long for neatness and order, this calling will undoubtedly be messy. The messiness of living, talking, and working with other humans is above all a result of personal and social sin in the world. The fall of humanity in the garden of Eden not only alienated humankind from God but also alienated us from one another. One of the foremost effects of sin is that certain humans will attempt to dominate and rule over other humans (Gen. 3:16). Even in the first generation after the fall, Cain and Abel are alienated from each other as Cain becomes jealous of Abel, eventually killing him.

Jealousy is a powerful force that continues to alienate us today. We constantly compare ourselves to others and long for more resources, more stuff, and more power. This situation is made worse by our inclination to greed—that is, our hesitancy to share our resources with others. If we have privilege and a wealth of resources, we are hesitant to share these assets with others who are not so privileged. Additionally, we are alienated from one another by our pride. We think we understand ourselves and others better than we actually do. Our pride inclines us to pigeonhole others into neat categories—Democrat, Republican, gay, affluent, homeless, Lutheran, Southerner, and so on—and to engage with them on the basis of stereotypes rather than doing the slow and challenging work of getting to know them.

Our pride similarly skews our understanding of the social and natural worlds within which we are embedded, warping our ability to have meaningful conversations with others, especially those who come from different backgrounds than we do. To protect ourselves from the searing effects of pride and the desire for power, we often learn to respond with distrust. If we get a whiff that someone has an inflated sense of their own knowledge or agenda, we are inclined to take a step back and attempt to protect ourselves with the tools of distrust, including skepticism and dismissiveness. As necessary as these measures might seem at the time, they serve only to widen the existing gaps between us.

Our Sunday night conversations at Englewood Christian Church were extremely volatile in their earliest years. Members yelled at and were fiercely sarcastic with one another. This volatility was fueled in large part by pride and a desire for the sort of power that came from controlling the direction of the conversation (and presumably the direction of the church as well). Many of us were proudly adamant that our convictions were right, and we defended them fiercely, even at times with sarcasm. It's not difficult to imagine why we had such difficulty talking with one another in those early years!

To say that the effects of pride and power are not present in our congregational conversations today would be naive. However, as we grow to know and trust one another better, we are learning to navigate these struggles more gracefully. Our knowledge of one another spurs us to trust one another in spite of the sinful desires of pride and power that lurk in each of our hearts. Our trust also helps us to be more conscious of our own pride and desire for power and to struggle to keep these forces in check, lest we unravel the trust that we have already cultivated with one another.

The effects of personal sin are compounded by social sin that has not only warped our formation as persons and communities but continues to warp our interactions with one another. When we bear the wounds of violence or injustice—due to gender, race, class, or ethnicity, for instance—it becomes difficult to converse with those who are part of the group responsible for inflicting those wounds on us. Racial and economic injustices play a major role in education, and those who are less privileged tend not to have access to better and higher education that lends nuance and insight into the sociopolitical realities within which we live. Injustices related to the environment, food, and health care impact the ability of some to participate consistently in church conversations; these same kinds of injustices can likewise impact the quality of participation by causing distractions that hinder one's ability to focus. If, for instance, you have a fierce toothache that goes untreated because you don't have dental insurance, the pain is going to affect your ability to follow and contribute meaningfully to conversation. Similarly, mental illness that goes untreated, or that is not treated well, will shape how those afflicted with it participate in conversations.

Over the last decade, the scientific and medical communities have become increasingly attentive to the effects of trauma. The science of epigenetics, for instance, indicates that some forms of trauma might even alter our genetic composition and thus be passed to future generations in our genes. Trauma warps our social, physical, and mental health, shaping the ways that we participate in conversations. Certain topics of conversation may be difficult or even impossible for us because they remind us of a previous trauma in some way and trigger responses of self-protection or exit from the conversation. Some trauma is the bitter fruit of social sin. War, for example, is traumatic both for those who are employed in waging it (we've learned a great deal in recent decades about the gruesome effects of PTSD on soldiers who have been in combat) and for the people in whose homeland it is being waged. Sexual or domestic violence is another traumatic effect of social and personal sin.

Other forms of trauma are less directly connected to sin and are simply the fruits of living in a broken creation. Although some natural disasters, such as the BP oil spill of 2010 in the Gulf of Mexico, clearly stem from human sin against creation, others—like hurricanes and tsunamis—are less clear in their origins but traumatic nonetheless.

Personal sin, social sin, and trauma all affect our capacity to participate rationally and clearheadedly in conversation. We may dodge (or be overly aggressive on) certain topics because of the pains that we or our loved ones have experienced. We may not even be conscious of how we respond, or even of the particular causes that initiate these responses.

Our Human Finitude

Sin and trauma are not the only factors that contribute to the messiness of our conversations. We are finite human beings, and as such, we live within particular limitations. Every human being is created uniquely in the image of God. We each have our set of gifts, experiences, and wounds, and we face a great temptation to become obsessed with our own lives: pursuing *my* personal dreams, grappling with *my* own brokenness, and trying to wrap *my* mind around the question of what it will look like for *me* to follow Jesus. Our self-absorption contributes significantly to the messiness of our life together and to our conversations as churches. In *Compassion*, Nouwen, McNeill, and Morrison astutely observe that

> paying attention to our fellow human beings is far from easy. We tend to be so insecure about our self-worth and so much in need of affirmation that it is very hard not to ask for attention ourselves. Before we are fully aware of it, we are speaking about ourselves, referring to our experiences, telling our stories, or turning the subject of conversation toward our own territory. . . . To pay attention

to others with the desire to make them the center and make their interests our own is a real form of self-emptying, since to be able to receive others into our intimate inner space, we must be empty. That is why listening is so difficult.[7]

As humans, we each have a unique formation and story, but we are never fully privy to the stories of others; and due to the fuzziness of memory, we likely are not even fully privy to our own past. We see life reflected to us—to paraphrase the apostle Paul—in a hazy mirror. We do not live in a relativistic world, as some postmodern thinkers suppose. In this world, there is indeed truth and reality, but the complicating factor is that we can never achieve complete certainty about what is true and real and what isn't. We yearn for the order that would be provided to us in certainty, for the clarity of separating good from evil; yet as ardently as we push for clarity, we never arrive at certainty.

Drawing on the work of twentieth-century philosopher Michael Polanyi, theologian Lesslie Newbigin has described our work of knowing the world around us as more like the ways that we know other human beings and less like the apparent certainty with which we know things in mathematics. In his important book *Proper Confidence: Faith, Doubt, and Certainty in Christian Discipleship*, Newbigin explains the nature of our knowing: "If we are to use the word 'certainty' . . . then it is not the [mathematical] certainty of Descartes. It is the kind of certainty expressed in such words as those of the Scriptures: 'I know whom I have believed, and I am sure that he is able to guard until that day what has been entrusted to me' (2 Tim. 1:12). Note here two features of this kind of assurance which distinguish it from the ideal of certainty that we have inherited from the Age of Reason."[8]

Newbigin goes on to note that it is not our own knowledge but rather the reliability of God our Maker that anchors our confidence. Furthermore, the apostle Paul's phrase "until that day" cautions us that we do not possess truth in all its fullness but need to be open to new ways God is leading us deeper into truth. Paul writes that God, "the one to whom [he is] committed, is able to bring [him] to the full grasp of what [he] now only partly understand[s]."⁹

Our work of knowing the world unfolds within particular communities rooted in historical traditions that orient us toward knowledge, first of the Creator and then of the creation. Newbigin writes:

> We are not given a theory which we then translate into practice. Instead, we are invited to respond to a word of calling by believing and acting, specifically by becoming part of the community which is already committed to the service of the Builder. We are invited to commit ourselves and to learn as we go what our role in the whole enterprise is to be. Our commitment is an act of personal faith. There is no possibility of the kind of indubitable certainty that Descartes claimed. . . . We are promised that as we so commit ourselves we shall be led step-by-step into a fuller understanding of the truth.¹⁰

The gap between how we have been formed (i.e., to expect certainty by the modern patterns of education in schools and churches) and the reality of our more personal ways of knowing (as described above by Newbigin) contributes greatly to the messiness of the situation we're in. We expect and long for neatness and certainty, and yet all we have to go on is the knowledge of our Creator and of our fellow human beings, both of whom can seem distant at times. We don't have certainty, but rather, as Newbigin argues, we have proper confidence that there is a Creator who longs to know us and to be known by us and who is slowly and gradually revealing the nature of God and of creation to us.

Our situation in the twenty-first century, and the personal way of knowing described by Newbigin, carries within it a paradox. On the one hand, our lack of certainty amplifies messiness in our conversations, but on the other hand, knowledge is only possible within a community that is striving to know and be known in conversation. Yes, as a result of sin, trauma, and our finitude, conversation will be extraordinarily messy, and yet apart from communities in conversation, we plunge deeper into the abyss of isolation and nihilism.

Being Together

One apparent shortcut around abiding together in messiness is to orient our conversations toward getting things done. Although I would never advocate for conversation apart from the daily sorts of decisions and actions that comprise our lives, our primary end in conversation should not be *doing* but *being*. "Being" as I am using it here refers to a larger focus within which doing is subsumed.

Although it may give us a sense of efficiency and allow us to steer clear of some messiness, to focus primarily on doing is to be too narrow in our vision and to sever our doing from the knowledge of one another, our neighbors, and our place, which is being built within our community. Many Westerners are formed by their workplaces, which are often keenly focused on productivity and unhealthily skewed toward doing. Conversations oriented primarily toward doing lead us into action that is, all too often, superficial and not sustainable. Meaningful and sustainable action flows from a conversation oriented toward being that takes into account both the deepest knowledge of the context within which the action occurs and the knowledge of those who will be involved in the action, of the gifts and resources that they bring to it, as well as their limitations, which will also shape the action. For almost a decade, beginning in the mid-1980s, our church ran an extensive charity ministry in our neighborhood. We had a food pantry, a clothing pantry, and even built a warehouse at the end of our parking lot to house a furniture pantry. We gave away a lot of stuff to neighbors in need, but we saw little transformation in terms of our relationships with the neighbors we served. In retrospect, we did not know our neighborhood well enough to know that it was oversaturated with charity ministries like ours. We also weren't fully cognizant of how our seeming generosity was being abused. Some neighbors, for instance, preferred to get free clothes from clothing pantries and then to dispose of them when they were dirty rather than paying the minimal cost to wash them. We were doing lots of things but not reflecting much on how or where they were being done. Eventually the pantries were shut down, but the church remained, and we soon found new and more attentive ways of relating to our neighbors. To the extent that our churches are able to make peace with our calling to *be* communities of God's people together in all the messiness of that calling, we will be able to act faithfully and sustainably in our neighborhoods and beyond.

Although we may take pains to avoid it, conversation will inevitably be messy; rather than trying to steer ourselves around that messiness, we would do better to learn to abide patiently in the midst of it. Broadening the focus of our conversations from doing to being will not only help us act more meaningfully; it will also create a space in which we are learning to be present to one another and to God, our Creator and Sustainer. Having been formed by the powers of modernity to favor efficiency and neatness and to hide any semblance of our own weakness, learning to abide in messy conversations will require significant work of us. In the following chapter, we explore that work in greater detail, focusing on the ways in which we prepare—or are prepared—to enter into it. Like any discipline, conversation goes best when we prepare our spirit, mind, and body for it.

7

Preparing Our Whole Selves
for Conversation

We must not force events, but rather make
The heart soil ready for their coming, as
The earth spreads carpets for the feet of Spring,
Or, with the strengthening tonic of the frost,
Prepares for Winter.

> —Ella Wheeler Wilcox, "Preparation"

Over the past half century, the culture of the United States has been dominated by consumerism. The acceleration of industry before and during World War II required new markets to sustain its growth. Increased production dovetailed with a boom in broadcast media—first radio, then television, and most recently the internet and social media—to seduce citizens into buying more stuff, often stuff we didn't really need. Consumerism tapped into the Western individualism that had been escalating during the last few centuries of the modern era.

Isolated from the wisdom and resource-sharing of community, the desires of individual consumers were easily manipulated into the constant desire for new, better, and more stuff.

Our churches have not been immune from the effects of this rampant consumerism. We are increasingly being formed by the larger culture to participate in church as consumers. We are inclined to evaluate church like we evaluate toothpaste or breakfast cereal—what is it doing *for me*? The worship service, the sermon, even various ministries of the church—youth ministry, children's ministry, men's or women's ministry—can all become products we consume for our individual spiritual health.

Comedian John Crist recently unmasked the consumerism in our churches in a hilarious video series titled *Church Hunters*. A parody of HGTV's show *House Hunters*, the series features Nick and Molly, a couple who recently moved to a new city and are on the hunt for a new church but can't exactly agree on what they want. "The church we go to now," says Nick at the outset of the series, "is just not doing it for us." An engaging pastor is one of the key ingredients on the couple's church shopping list. Molly chimes in, "We're looking for the humor of Andy Stanley with the body of Steven Furtick." The show's host, Corey, introduces the couple to a new church in each episode. Episode 1 features Creekside First Baptist, which "while it is traditional, is still pretty current." Creekside's building has a lot of side exits, for those who might need to slip out of the service early. Ultimately, Creekside turns out to be too traditional for Nick and Molly. The pastor's main point, Nick notes, was too long to be tweetable. Corey slyly dodges Molly's question about whether Creekside allows women to serve in ministry roles.

In episode 2, the couple is introduced to Molded Clay Jar Art Tapestry Canvas Mosaic Church, which as one might expect with an absurd name like that, "takes relevance to a whole new level." Not surprisingly, this church is full of celebrities. The couple agrees that they are looking for an inspirational service that is like "a TED talk with a Bible verse." Although the church has five services, held throughout the day every Sunday, the couple is irked that there is no midafternoon service, which is the best time of the day for them. Although they like it better than Creekside, the couple ends up split on their opinions about this more contemporary church. Molly thinks they could make it work, but Nick is irritated that he emailed the pastor and didn't get an immediate reply from him.

Like most good comedy, *Church Hunters* melds its laughs with incisive truths, particularly truths about how consumerism shapes our faith in the twenty-first century. In order to be healthy bodies, our churches need to make the shift from consumption to participation. "What does this church have to offer me?" should not be the first question on our minds but, rather, "What do I have to offer to this church?"

In 1 Corinthians, the apostle Paul describes the church in Corinth as a participatory church in which members come prepared to teach, sing, speak in tongues, or interpret for those who have spoken in tongues. In fact, the Corinthians' problem is that their gathering becomes chaotic in the flurry of everyone wanting to share and in the disorder of people who speak in tongues with no one volunteering to interpret (1 Cor. 14). In the latter half of the chapter, Paul instructs the church to be orderly in their participation together. Those who are led to speak should do so in turn, and if they speak in tongues, another member should interpret their message (14:27).

Conversation is by nature participatory. Even when we are not speaking, we participate by listening carefully and by weighing in our minds what is said. If a gathering is not open for participation, it is not conversation. Passively listening to a podcast, a panel discussion, or even a sermon—as beneficial as each of these might be in certain contexts—is not conversation. The key to making the shift from a church life centered on consumption to one centered on participation is the practice of preparation.

In this chapter, we will examine some crucial ways we prepare ourselves to contribute to our church's conversations. Like many North American churches, my church has been deeply formed by the forces of consumerism, but through our practices of conversation, we strive to be more participatory. We kept this desire to become more participatory in mind when we wrote our church covenant several years ago. One of the commitments we included was that we each would "honor God's presence and respect the time and effort of our sisters and brothers by attending as much as is reasonably possible, and by diligently using our gifts to prepare for and to enrich our time together."[1] God is still at work transforming us, but our commitments to attend and to prepare orient us toward a more participatory life together. As we seek to participate together in the singular body of Christ, we would do well to reflect on the ways that we each prepare our hearts, our minds, and our bodies to participate in conversation together.

Preparing Our Hearts

In the Western tradition, one's heart is understood metaphorically as the seat of one's desires. Consumerism preys on many of our self-oriented desires: to look or feel good (or at least to look *better* than those around us). To prepare our hearts for conversation is to reflect seriously on our desires, to ask ourselves what it is that we really, really want. Do we want to see God's reign come on earth as it is in heaven? Or are we more interested in looking or feeling good, or in acquiring things that promise to make us healthier, happier, or more secure?

Prayer plays a vital role in preparing our hearts for conversation. In prayer we ask God to change our desires. "Your kingdom come," we pray as Jesus taught us, and in these words we submit our desires for the building of our personal empires to the larger work of God's transformation of the world. Devoting time to being in God's presence in prayer and seeking God's transformation of our hearts so that we might yearn for God's reign will prepare us to know God's presence and guidance in our conversations. It will also give us courage to follow God's lead as we talk together, even when the conversation gets contentious.

In one of the most striking passages in Richard Foster's classic book *Celebration of Discipline*, he shows readers how they might prepare themselves for worship. Foster's guidance is equally helpful as we consider how we might prepare our hearts for conversation. The ancient Israelites, Foster notes, gathered with a holy expectancy that they would hear the very voice of God, the *kol Yahweh*. The same was true of the early Christian communities. When they gathered, they "were coming into the awful, glorious, gracious presence of the living God. They gathered with anticipation, knowing that Christ was present among them and would teach them and touch them with his living power."[2]

How do we cultivate a holy expectancy similar to that which guided God's people in Scripture and throughout the intervening centuries? Foster offers some practical wisdom. He suggests that we first learn to expect God's presence with us throughout the whole week. If we are ever-expectant to know God's presence, then certainly we will know it in our gathering as the body of Christ. In addition to learning to desire God's continual presence with us, Foster challenges us to use our imaginations to anticipate God's presence with us. His guidance for preparing for worship services is strikingly applicable to our gatherings for conversation:

Enter the [gathering space] ten minutes early. Lift your heart in adoration to the King of glory. Contemplate his majesty, glory, and tenderness as revealed in Jesus Christ. Picture the marvelous vision that Isaiah had of the Lord "high and lifted up" or the magnificent revelation that John had of Christ with eyes "like a flame of fire" and voice "like the sound of many waters" (Isa. 6; Rev. 1). Invite the real Presence to be manifest.

Next, lift into the light of Christ [the facilitator of your conversation and all who will speak]. Picture the Shekinah of God's radiance surrounding them. Inwardly release them to speak the truth boldly in the power of the Lord.

When people begin to enter the room, glance around until you see someone who needs your intercessory work. Perhaps their shoulders are drooped, or they seem a bit sad. Lift them into the glorious, refreshing light of his Presence.[3]

Another vital question we must ask ourselves as we prepare our hearts for conversation is, Do we *really* desire to be united with our brothers and sisters in the body of Christ? Or would we prefer to persist as an autonomous individual? In the Sermon on the Mount, Jesus instructs his disciples, "So when you are offering your gift at the altar, if you remember that your brother or sister has something against you, leave your gift there before the altar and go; first be reconciled to your brother or sister, and then come and offer your gift" (Matt. 5:23–24). Similarly, if we know that someone in our congregation has something against us, we should approach them before our gathering for conversation and try to be reconciled. Our failure to be reconciled with one another will affect the shape and direction of our conversations. A lack of reconciliation can lead to bitterness, which in turn can severely impact our communication with that person. For instance, bitterness can lead us to not listen to this person or to assume the worst about what he or she says. If there are multiple people in a group who have not been reconciled to one another, conversation will become increasingly strained. To paraphrase the apostle John, if we desire to love, to know, and to be reconciled to God (whom we have not seen), then we must learn to love, to know, and to be reconciled to our sisters and brothers, whom we have seen (1 John 4:20). Reconciliation might not always be possible, but if we desire reconciliation and are talking with the person with whom we are at odds and are working toward reconciliation, that will be sufficient preparation for us as we enter into our conversations together.

Preparing Our Minds

In addition to preparing our hearts for conversation, we also need to prepare our minds. Reading is one important means by which our minds are prepared. Sometimes a facilitator might announce a particular reading—a portion of Scripture, a chapter from a book, or even a short story—that can serve as preparation for an upcoming conversation. If a preparatory reading of this sort is announced, we should make every effort to read it carefully and well, reflecting on its significance to the central questions of the upcoming conversation.

Our conversation will especially benefit if at least some people have read not only the recommended passage but other pertinent materials as well. If a passage of Scripture is recommended, for instance, perhaps one might read additional chapters before and after the passage for context that will assist in understanding the recommended passage. If, for instance, the suggested reading is a chapter from Galatians, one might read the whole epistle. If the recommended reading is not a scriptural passage, one might read other related pieces by the same author. If the reading is a chapter from a book, and you have access to a copy of the book, you might find an additional chapter or chapters that seem relevant to the upcoming conversation. If the recommended passage mentions or cites other works that you have access to, these might also serve as pertinent prereading. Another way to uncover related materials is to do an internet search for the author(s) of the recommended prereading, along with one or more keywords that are central to the topic of conversation. We should also be sensitive to the fact that our congregations will have people who struggle with reading. For their sake, we might also recommend some preparatory materials in other media formats: videos, podcasts, or other recordings, for instance.

Using these methods, we will be sure to find more than enough materials to prepare our minds for the upcoming conversation. An overabundance of pertinent resources can be intimidating, though. How can we prepare our minds for conversation in a way that is joyful, refreshing, and not overwhelming? The key to answering this question is found in being attentive to our passions and curiosities. If some facet of the upcoming conversation is of particular interest to me, I will try to read as much as possible in that vein. Given that any group will include people with a variety of passions and interests, following one's interests and curiosities in preparing will ensure a good range of diverse perspectives on the conversational topic and interconnected topics.

Sometimes we find ourselves preparing our minds by reading in ways that aren't as intentional as those described above. We might be reading something—say, a novel, a passage of Scripture, or an online news article—purely for our own interests, and we discover a connection with a recent or upcoming topic of conversation. If this reading sufficiently piques our interest, it might lead to others in a manner similar to that described above (reading related works that are mentioned, searching the internet for related materials, etc.). The deeper we get in our conversations, the more they will weigh on our minds; as a result, connections to the conversation will manifest themselves abundantly in things we are reading or in our everyday experiences.

In addition to reading, another practice that cultivates connections and helps us to remember them is note-taking. For many of us, note-taking has a negative connotation that stems from our experience with it in our schooling. The sort of note-taking that will benefit our conversations is a different sort than what we learned in school, in part because we will not be tested on the material that we cover in our conversations together. Slavish note-taking is not the goal and can in fact be a severe impediment to our learning to be present and attentive to one another. Note-taking should be a tool that aids our attentiveness rather than detracting from it.

Some people have the agility of mind and hand to take robust notes while remaining present with others in the conversation. Indeed, in our age of severe attention deficits, taking notes can be a vital way for some people to stay focused and engaged in the conversation. Some participants will find it helpful to jot down many, if not all, of the key ideas and questions that the conversation raises. Others will be more selective in their note-taking, only jotting down thoughts that are especially striking to them: a thought that stood out because of its elegant articulation, a point that was unsettling and would merit further reflection, or a question that the group keeps bumping up against and never sufficiently answers, for example. Others may function best by not taking notes at all during the conversation but later writing down a question or two that held particular interest for them and that they will want to explore in further detail. Each person will have to decide what form of note-taking works best for them. Balancing the aims of being present to others in the conversation and recording key thoughts and questions in order to inscribe them more deeply in our memory, keeping them at the forefront of our minds throughout the intervening time until our next conversation, is the desired end.

Here at Englewood Christian Church, we assign one person to be the official notetaker for each of our Sunday conversations. Similar to our facilitator role, the notetaker role is assigned beforehand, and his or her primary function on that day is not to contribute to the conversation but to take notes. Assigning a notetaker does not mean that we discourage others from taking notes; rather, it allows us to distribute the notes to anyone who might not have been able to attend the conversation—thus helping them prepare for the next conversation. It also helps us keep a record of our conversations that can be referenced in the future.

As we prepare for upcoming conversations, reading and note-taking are practices that help us to reflect continually on the central questions of that conversation. Sometimes, we will need to create time and space in our lives for intentional reflection as we prepare. These times of reflection might include reading and rereading our notes from previous conversations, along with any notes that we might have taken from readings that we have done in preparation. The aim of our reflection should be clarity and cultivating new connections in our minds that help us better understand the topic of conversation. Reflection helps us order our thoughts. What are the most important, or the most troubling, questions related to the topic at hand? What other thoughts and questions are interesting but less important? How does the conversational topic affect the shape of our very lives as we seek to follow Jesus in this community of God's people. Are there particular terms that have been used in the conversation that seem problematic to us, and if so, why? What aspects of the life and teaching of Jesus do we see emerging in our conversation? These questions and many related ones can help us to reflect on the meaning and direction of our conversation and to prepare our minds to participate in coming conversations.

Another beneficial practice of reflection is to have necessary conversations *before the conversation*. If someone has said something in the previous conversation that you don't understand or agree with, and if the flow of conversation doesn't get around to unpacking this statement, it would be helpful to follow up with this person in an effort to understand them more clearly. Not only can this practice be a vital step toward the sort of reconciliation described earlier in this chapter; it can also help us fuel new thoughts for reflection as we prepare our minds for conversation. At our church, these conversations before the conversation often take the form of people continuing to engage one another immediately *after* our formal time of conversation has ended. It is not unusual for these informal conversations to extend for another hour or two after we have dismissed the group conversation.

Reflection on our church's conversation serves the crucial role of orienting our minds toward the transforming life of God in the midst of our community. If we believe that Scripture is the primary story that gives meaning to our lives, and if our primary allegiance is to the new creation that God has established in Jesus, then these things should saturate our minds and lives as we work and care for our church and our families in other ways. The sort of preparation that I have described here, when pursued earnestly with a desire to love God and love our neighbors, can serve to be the renewing of our minds that the apostle Paul maintains will be transformative (Rom. 12:1–2), not only shaping the ways that we imagine, think about, and talk about the world but also transforming how we live within it. By talking about the ways in which God is leading us together as a church and by working diligently to reflect on these conversations, we are doing theology, not in an abstract, disconnected sense, but in a way that is rooted in the particular realities within which our community lives and moves and has its being. Our deeply engaged participation in these conversations will infuse us with the hope that the new creation of God is not only possible but already emerging in the shared life of our church community.

Preparing Our Bodies

Our hearts and minds are interwoven with our bodies, and it will be beneficial for us to prepare our bodies for conversation as well. While good nutrition and general physical fitness will significantly contribute to our health and well-being in ways that benefit our conversations, that is not the sort of bodily preparation that I want to explore here. Rather, the two more important types of bodily preparation that I want to highlight are the training of our eyes and ears for attentiveness and the benefits of rest for our conversations.

If, as I have argued here, the primary end of our conversations is to be present to God and one another, then it will be essential for us to cultivate habits that make this end possible. The twenty-first century is an age of distraction, and paying attention can be particularly difficult for us in this age. We need practices that help us train our eyes and ears to be more attentive, and these practices may vary widely from person to person. One person may prefer to listen carefully to jazz or classical music, to hear the intricate ways in which instruments or voices are beautifully orchestrated in a particular piece of music. Another may go to a local art museum or gallery and spend large chunks of time taking in the colors, textures, and shapes of a particular piece of art. A third person may prefer to read poetry, slowly breathing out the words of a poem, trying to understand the poet's intent and to imagine vividly the image that the poet is conveying in a particular work.

Theologian Philip Kenneson tells his students at the liberal arts college where he teaches that the most important course they might take is Vertebrate Field Biology, informally known as the bird-watching class. Why bird watching? Kenneson explains:

> [Bird watching] trains you to pay exquisite attention to something that has always been right in front of you.
>
> You discover the subtle differences between different kinds of warblers, thrushes, and sparrows. You find out that they all have names and unique songs. All of a sudden, you begin to see, really see, these birds all the time. And you begin to hear their songs, their amazing music, not because they weren't there to see or hear before, but because you had never really paid attention before.
>
> And for many students, this is a revelation. An epiphany if you will. It opens up a whole new world, and the new world it opens is not just about birds. Because once you learn how to pay attention to the glory of birds, birds that have always been there, you begin

to wonder what else you've been missing, what else you haven't been paying attention to.[4]

Just as following your passions and curiosities is beneficial while reading in preparation for conversation, following our passions is vital—life giving—as we choose practices that help train our eyes and ears to be more attentive. Our increasing attentiveness will be a significant asset to the conversations we have as a church. We cultivate this attentiveness in our daily and weekly rhythms, so when we participate in conversation, our attention to detail is second nature.

Although there is a growing body of literature over recent years on the benefits of rest and Sabbath for human well-being,[5] I won't dive into that work here, except to make one observation. The exhaustion that most of us face from trying to keep up with an ever-accelerating world is a significant impediment to our capacity to be attentive and to relate graciously to one another. Preparing ourselves for conversation by getting decent rest—or at least not teetering on the brink of utter exhaustion—contributes to our church's capacity to have meaningful conversations.

In our breakneck world, how is it possible for us to be better rested for our conversations? First, rest should be one crucial factor in deciding when we are going to gather for conversation as a church. When is a suitable time in which most of our active members could be rested and ready for conversation? In most church settings, the congregation is *not* likely to be well rested immediately after a worship service. For some churches that worship together on Sunday mornings, gathering for conversation on Sunday evenings might be one time when members can be sufficiently rested and ready for conversation.

On a personal level, each of us should endeavor to get a reasonable amount of rest on a daily basis. For some people, their jobs or family situations (e.g., parents with very young children) may make getting good rest a challenge. If we are caring well for one another, we will be able to help these restless ones to get a bit of rest—watching young children or taking on helpful tasks that allow that person to rest a little. Sometimes getting adequate rest requires forgoing some entertainment—"just one more television episode," for instance. Working to get the rest we need will not only benefit our conversations but will also help us be more attentive and gracious in all situations of our everyday life.

A Culture of Preparation

Although each of us should be doing the needed work to prepare our hearts, minds, and bodies for our conversations, our personal preparations are reinforced when our church community has a culture in which preparation is normative and expected. In a consumer society that poses significant challenges to such a culture—as we explored earlier in this chapter—how do we begin to cultivate this sort of culture of preparation? First, we need congregational leaders who lead by their example in preparing for our conversations. If we have leaders who consistently do *not* prepare, then it will be exponentially more difficult for us to achieve a culture of preparation.

In addition to leaders who model preparation, we can move toward a culture of preparation by teaching it as part of catechesis, our training of new members. It is vital that we teach potential members the basic convictions and doctrines that give shape to our life as a church. The historic tradition of catechesis, however, not only prepared the minds of new members but also introduced them to essential practices of the church. If conversation is an essential practice in the life of our church, then it would be transformative to introduce new members to this practice and especially how (and why) our members prepare to participate in conversation. Especially given the prevalence of individualism and consumerism in Western society, we will need this sort of intentionality as we train new members to participate in—and not just consume the fruits of—our life together in the local church.

One of the most important factors in sustaining practices of conversation is the formation of congregational culture in the shape of the sort of spirituality that I have described here— prayerful, capable of abiding in messiness, and willing to do the necessary work in preparation for conversations. In the final part of this book, we will look at other factors that enable us to sustain our practices of conversation even through difficult and contentious seasons.

PART 3

SUSTAINING THE JOURNEY

8

Cultivating a Sense
of Mission and Identity

When we lose our myths we lose our place in the universe.
—Madeleine L'Engle, *The Rock That Is Higher*

The book of Acts is a story of a body in motion, specifically the body of Christ. From the earliest days after the ascension of Jesus, his followers are in motion, following the lead of the Holy Spirit, sharing resources, praying together, and eventually proclaiming the good news in Judea, Samaria, and to the ends of the Roman Empire. Before he ascended, Jesus foretold that his disciples would bear witness to his life and work, and the first-century church took this proclamation—along with the teachings of the apostles, who had shared life with Jesus and knew him most intimately—as central to their mission, the work into which they had been called.

One of the greatest threats to the churches of the first century, as we read in Acts and most of the New Testament epistles, was the struggle of Jewish and gentile Christians to live together in the united body of Christ. At the heart of the book of Acts, in chapter 15, lies a story of this kind of struggle. After crisscrossing the eastern regions of the Roman Empire, Paul and Barnabas settled in for a stay in Antioch, the home of one of the most thriving churches of that day. While Paul and Barnabas were in Antioch, some Jewish Christians came down from Judea, announcing that "unless you are circumcised according to the custom of Moses, you cannot be saved" (Acts 15:1). In essence, these Jews were saying that in order to follow Christ, gentiles would need to become Jews first, taking the traditional defining mark of circumcision on their bodies. This struggle was largely one for the control of God's people: Who would dictate how the church should live their faith and bear witness to the gospel? Paul and Barnabas reacted vehemently to these Jewish teachers, having "no small dissension and debate with them" (v. 2). A group of church leaders, including Paul and Barnabas, were chosen to go to Jerusalem and discuss this issue with the apostles and elders of the church there.

At the gathering in Jerusalem, the apostle Peter proclaims that he is the one through whom God initially extended the invitation to gentiles to enter into the people of God. The same Holy Spirit, Peter preaches, was given to the gentiles as was given to the Jews in Jerusalem at Pentecost. Jews and gentiles alike are loved by God and saved by the grace of God, not by their actions. Later James turns the attention of the gathering to the teachings of the prophets who had foretold God's plan for gentiles to be invited into God's people, the house of David. Asserting that it seemed "good to us and to the Holy Spirit," the assembly decides that Jewish and gentile Christians should "abstain only from things polluted by idols and from fornication and from whatever has been strangled and from blood" (Acts 15:20). Circumcision is not to be mandated as an identifying mark of the Christian. Although the Jews were the first ones chosen by God, they are not to be overlords in the people of God; they are not to be forever the arbiters of Christian faithfulness. The church in Jerusalem writes a letter of encouragement to their sister church in Antioch, explaining this decision, and sends Paul, Barnabas, and a delegation of leaders to deliver it. Reading the letter brings much joy to the church in Antioch (v. 31), but circumcision and other tensions between Jewish and gentile Christians would continue to plague churches throughout the first century.

This crucial story from Acts 15 can be helpful for us as we seek to be faithful in the twenty-first century and cultivate practices of conversation. This story, of course, unfolds in a series of conversations—first between the contentious Jewish advocates of circumcision and the dissenting Paul and Barnabas; then among Paul, Barnabas, and the apostles and elders of Jerusalem; and finally, back in Antioch as the news of the Jerusalem church's decision is announced. Perhaps even more important than the account of these conversations is their trajectory and *how* this struggle in the first-century churches ultimately unites God's people instead of tearing them apart. Rather than focusing on the conflict that arose around circumcision (I will explore conflict and conflict resolution in the next chapter), in this chapter I will explore how cultivating a rich sense of mission and identity can sustain our conversations, as it sustained those of the early Christians in this story from Acts.

How did this sense of identity and mission among the early Christians sustain them through these tense conversations? In spite of their diverse ethnic heritages (Jews and a wide range of gentiles), the Christians understood themselves as belonging to a single people, namely the people of God. This belonging was central to their identity. I will explore the role of a robust sense of peoplehood in more detail in chapter 10, but I mention it here because the notion of peoplehood is essential in any coherent conversation about identity and mission. Although we may have diverse convictions about our identity and mission—as the Jews and gentiles did on the issue of circumcision—seeing ourselves as united in Christ's body compels us to take stock of divergences such as these and to wrestle with them in light of who we are (identity) and the work into which God has called us (mission).

Every People Has a Story

From ancient times to the present day, every society has a complex, multilayered story that gives shape and meaning to how they live in the world. Ancient peoples—Egyptians, Babylonians, Greeks, and Romans, for instance—had their mythologies that explained how the world came into being, where it was headed, and how they should live within it. In the present secular age, we are still driven by mythologies. The primary actors in our myths are not anthropomorphic gods as they were for the ancients but, rather, nebulous forces like the nation-state and the market. These forces narrate for us a way of living in the world that is driven by substories like individualism, consumerism, and militarism. Our mythology explains how we have come to be as a people and how we should live in order to sustain our peoplehood.

In the United States the mythology of democracy has been a driving story throughout our history. The idea that the general populace can and should participate in the governance of their nation is woven deeply into our formation, in everything from regular cycles of presidential and congressional elections to the prominent role of the press to our judicial right to challenge legislation. Even when the majority of our population was not allowed to vote, the democratic virtue of equality guided us into eras in which women and people of color were granted the right to vote. Democracy is a mythology that has led us into wars to resist totalitarianism in order to, in the ambitious words of Woodrow Wilson, make the world "safe for democracy."[1]

Manifest Destiny is another central myth that has shaped and continues to shape the people of the United States. This myth, which drove the expansion of the American empire across the

North American continent, around the globe, and even into space, has been reincarnated during the last century as one of the fundamental substories of consumerism: we should never be content but always driven by the quest for more, bigger, and better stuff. Now that the vast majority of the land across our nation has been consumed, Manifest Destiny has shifted its object to material goods, but the mythology driving the consumption remains the same.

In the Christian tradition, our guiding story is provided in Scripture. In this collection of writings from diverse genres, we uncover a defining story about how and why the world was created, about the end toward which it is moving, and about how we should live as a people within this story. As Western culture becomes increasingly post-Christian, many churches struggle with members who have little familiarity with the contours of Scripture as a single story that enfolds the whole of human history. Our efforts to identify ourselves as a community whose common life emerges from the story of Scripture will help us to sustain practices of conversation. Scripture itself, consisting of sixty-six diverse books written over the course of many centuries, is a conversation into which we are immersed. The authors and characters of the scriptural story frequently converse with one another: Jesus quoting the prophets or Peter being hesitant to eat gentile food in the house of Cornelius on the basis of the Law, for instance. Even the canon of books that has been passed down to us emerged from intense conversations in the early church about which books merited inclusion in Scripture.

Among our Jewish ancestors in the faith, the scriptural story was intimately tied to the tradition of midrash, an ongoing conversation about the interpretation of scriptural texts. To live as part of God's people was to wade into the river of conversation about Scripture and what it means to live faithfully within God's story. For all the deep disagreements we might have about interpretations of Scripture within our congregations, we are a people defined by a single story about the world and how it works—that is, Scripture. Everything that we can do—from the cradle to the grave—to proclaim that Scripture is our primary story and to immerse ourselves daily in it will provide us with a firm bedrock on which to have conversations together, conversations through which we can imagine and construct our life as a people.

Immersing ourselves in the scriptural story is not simply a matter of teaching Scripture; many churches do that. *How* we teach Scripture matters. The Bible is not just a dusty history book or a book of moral teachings; it is the one story that gives meaning and order to our lives. Every person has a story (or we could say, a mythology) that shapes their lives—one story by which all others are weighed and interpreted. For some people that story is the American mythology; for others, it is consumerism. For us in the church, our story should the one told in Scripture. The challenge then is to teach Scripture in a way that allows it to come alive for us, causing us to increasingly see ourselves as belonging to its story. Those who preach and teach in our church—whether they teach toddlers or adults or anyone in between—should have a passion for living as part of God's people and should be able to communicate in at least basic ways how Scripture gives life and form to us as the church.

In addition to regularly teaching Scripture, special events throughout the church year can reinforce our identity as God's people located within the scriptural story. Every year the ancient Israelite people had a cycle of feasts that helped them remember the ways God had guided them throughout their history. Each feast told a particular story that was essential to the formation of Israel's identity as the people of God. Passover, or Pesach, for instance, celebrates of how God liberated the ancient Israelites from their slavery in Egypt. The feast of Purim celebrates how God saved Israel from Haman's intentions to kill all the Jews, a story recounted in the biblical book of Esther. The Jewish people see their life in the present as intimately connected with this history; it is their story.

In recent years our church in Indianapolis has established a tradition on Holy Saturday—the day before Easter—of walking through our garden and of listening to gifted storytellers guide us through the scriptural story, from creation to the death of Jesus. This journey reminds us of the unity of Scripture, a single story of God's love for creation, which is our story as it was also the story of Israel and the story of our ancestors in the Christian faith. Likewise, we observe the seasons of Advent, reflecting on the meaning of God's drawing near to us in Jesus, and of Lent, remembering Jesus's suffering and death. These seasons, which are not celebrated in many sister churches within our particular church tradition, orient us to the story of Scripture and form us into the life of Christ.

As we seek to immerse ourselves in the scriptural story, we must remember that it serves to form us into a contrast society, a people whose way of living and being offers a compelling alternative to the mainstream culture in which it exists. The Torah, the law of the ancient Israelites, formed them as a holy—that is, set apart—people who stood in contrast to the pagan nations who surrounded them. The Sermon on the Mount and the whole of Jesus's teachings orient us toward being a people who are distinctly different from the self-absorption, violence, and greed of the wider culture.

Too often preaching and teaching in our churches involves presenting nuggets of scriptural wisdom and sending our people out to live their lives under the prevailing stories of Western individualism and consumerism. This tendency often begins in our Sunday school classrooms when we teach biblical characters like Moses and David as superheroes. In his provocative book *The World Is Not Ours to Save*, Tyler Wigg-Stevenson observes that seeing biblical characters as superheroes quickly morphs into seeing ourselves as superheroes. It is at this point that things go terribly wrong, as we are decidedly not the heroes of the scriptural story.[2] When we teach Scripture in this way, we dilute it, and we fail to invite people into a new and different story. Certainly we have all been formed by the powers of individualism, and we continue to be formed by them—just as the ancient Israelites were enamored with their pagan neighbors (recall the story of 1 Sam. 8, for instance, in which Israel demands a king *like those who rule the pagan nations*). In spite of the temptations to follow in the ways of the world and our inclination to succumb to them, we must always remember that our story is guiding us in a different direction: we are being formed by God into a people that stands in sharp contrast to the ways of the world.

To the extent that we can teach Scripture as an overarching story that unites us and orients us toward being a contrast society, our ability to converse together will be improved. We may have conflicting interpretations within our congregation of what Scripture means for us, as the early Christians did in Acts 15, but we are united in our seeking to live within this story. The life into which we have been called is, above all, God's story. It is not the Jews' story or the gentiles' story, the conservatives' story or the progressives' story. It is God's story, and we all have been invited into it. Our desire to live faithfully within this scriptural story may help sustain us through seasons of tense disagreement.

In addition to the scriptural story, which describes the world as a whole, every local church has its own particular story: the traditions, decisions, and people who have formed its identity. A local church in the United Methodist tradition today might not only have inherited the forms of John Wesley and the Methodists but might at one time also have been a United Brethren church, a denomination that merged with the Methodists in the 1960s. This congregation, like many in the United Brethren tradition, may largely have consisted in its earliest days of German immigrants. This German heritage likely left an imprint on the congregation today, over a century after its founding. Fifty years ago, this congregation may have had a pastor or a group of lay leaders who were passionate about caring for the poor, and this passion might be one that the congregation has retained and that gives shape to their life together in the twenty-first century.

Owning the story of our congregation—our faithfulness as well as our unfaithfulness—can be a powerful force that sustains our habits of conversation. Knowing our congregation's story and working within it binds us together with the other members of our church community. Within our particular story, we are faced with the work of discerning what this story means. What are the acts of Christian faithfulness that we should remember and be energized by? What are the acts of unfaithfulness of which we need to repent? As we explored in chapter 6, history can be messy, not easily judged as faithful or unfaithful. We may have done faithful things for unfaithful reasons, or vice versa. Even in situations of overwhelming unfaithfulness, we may discern glimmers of faith. As with our reading of Scripture, we will likely be faced with competing interpretations of various threads of our church's story. Regardless, our story is a glue that binds us together. Our unity in owning this story, identifying as one community of people defined by this story, can help us sustain our conversations through seasons of apathy or conflict.

Maintaining Our Identity

The identity of our particular local church is a confluence of stories: the story of God's work in creation as told in Scripture, most importantly, but also the broader historical story of God's work in the church and the story of our particular congregation. We need habits of taking these stories seriously, as well as habits of discerning the direction in which they will flow as we move into the future. To be attentive to these stories we need agents of memory,[3] those who recall specific threads of faithfulness or unfaithfulness from one or more of these stories that are relevant to the specific situation in which we presently find ourselves. Ever since the time of René Descartes, who famously endeavored to set aside his knowledge of everything that had gone before him, the modern age has been marked by its aversion to history, and memory. Four hundred years later, this resistance to history has become commonplace. Too often, we have forgotten the stories of those who have gone before us: in our families, in our places, and in our faith.

In Wendell Berry's somewhat autobiographical novella *Remembering*, Andy Catlett moves from his home in rural Port William, Kentucky, to a big city.[4] Eventually, he wearies of urban life and moves back to Port William, where he seeks to be re-membered—reconnected as a functioning member of the people and the place. This basic plotline offers wisdom for our local churches. We may have spent our season away in the big city of modernity, so to speak, but our survival now hinges on our capacity to remember—to reconnect to the stories and the wisdom of those who have gone before us—and to draw on these memories to illuminate our way in the present and into the future.

Ancient philosophers wrestled with a question sometimes referred to as Theseus's paradox: How could an object retain its identity as its parts were replaced over time? Common contemporary wisdom, for example, tells us that every seven years all the cells in our body are replaced. While recent science has debunked the seven-year time frame, it confirms that almost all cells in the human body are regenerated at some point. Cells in some parts of the body are regenerated rapidly: the cells of our stomach lining, for instance, are replaced every four to nine days. Cells in other parts of the body may take twenty-five years or more to regenerate. It is a testimony to the memory and conversational power of our bodies that our identity is retained through constant cycles of regenerating cells. The memory of who I am as a person is passed in a conversation of sorts from older cells to newer ones.

Given our present aversion to history, one of the greatest challenges facing our churches is having a memory and an identity that roots us amid the howling storms of crises in our deeply fragmented age. Memory will undoubtedly serve as an anchor in our most tempestuous conversations, but how do we remember well? How do we remind ourselves of the stories—of Scripture, of the breadth and depth of God's work in the church, of our denomination (or nondenominational tradition), and of our local congregation—that help us retain our identity in the face of ever-changing members and ever-changing times?

In the mid-1990s, Phinney Ridge Lutheran Church in Seattle established a catechumenate, a conversational process for orienting potential members to the way of Christ in their particular congregation. This program, which spans the better part of a year, from fall until Pentecost, is a structure that helps the church have particular kinds of conversations together and demonstrates to potential members how to participate in the conversational life of their church. Each candidate is paired with a sponsor, an existing member of the church, and together they go through the program. A sponsor and candidate may connect during the week, and each weekend they participate in a gathering of all sponsors and candidates. The gathering begins with a meal, after which participants spend significant time reading and discussing the passage of Scripture that will be the focus of the next Sunday's worship service. The Scripture passage is read in a *lectio divina* format that invites conversation with the text and with a small group of others. This immersive catechumenate process has been wildly successful in forming new members for participation in that church body. Candidates who complete the process, ultimately becoming church members, are often eager to become sponsors of new candidates in subsequent years. Although the primary end of the catechumenate is church membership, one of the other benefits is that Phinney Ridge's members are learning to talk and to work together—often across generations—building relationships that help propagate their identity and work as the church.

Remembering the Story of God's Work in History

Reconnecting to the scriptural story begins with preachers and teachers who consistently teach Scripture, not as a dusty book of history or as a basket of wise morsels from which we can each draw as we live our individual lives but, rather, as a single story in which our church community (together with all our ancestors in the faith) is enmeshed. Good preaching and teaching will help us see ourselves in ancient Israel, in the disciples of Jesus, in the churches of the first century that were the recipients of the New Testament epistles, and in our church ancestors over the past two millennia. Our desires and our struggles bear a striking resemblance to those of our biblical ancestors. Like ancient Israel, we are probably more unfaithful than we are faithful. Like Jesus's disciples, we want the most prestigious fruits of God's kingdom for ourselves (e.g., to sit at the right and left hand of Jesus). Like the Jewish Christians of the early church, who operated from a place of privilege, we become so attached to our traditions that we cannot see the transforming hand of God at work. Too often, our motivating desire is to force others into our traditions or, if they resist these traditions, to banish them from the people of God.

Celebrating at least some of the seasons, feasts, and fasts that have provided rhythms for the people of God throughout the centuries is another powerful way to remember the scriptural story. Included in this are Advent and Lent, which increasing numbers of churches celebrate today, and also All Saints' Day, a time to celebrate the faithfulness of our ancestors, and perhaps even some of the holy days of the ancient Israelites, such as the Sabbath or Sukkot (the Feast of Booths), for instance.

Church of the Servant King in Eugene, Oregon, celebrates a cycle of feasts throughout the year that reminds them of their identity as a community of God's people. Some of their feasts are familiar ones from the church calendar, including Advent, Holy Week and Easter, and Pentecost. One of the less traditional feasts is their Celebration of the Faithful, which occurs during the week of All Saints' Day. This feast celebrates the faithful ones from the history of their congregation and the broader history of the church. "Using Hebrews 11:1–12:2 as a springboard," notes one member, "we take the week to hear from one another or from guests as they share about other people significant to their discipleship."[5] Their celebration also involves a healthy dose of frivolity, including dressing up like a character and telling that person's story of faithfulness. They have fun together, which serves to reinforce these stories of Christian faithfulness in their imaginations. Holiday celebrations like this one are a joyous and winsome way to remember our faith tradition. Any time a new holiday is introduced in our church community, it should be accompanied with teaching that identifies it not merely as a new practice but as a way of remembering, of connecting to the scriptural story of those who have gone before us in the faith.

Another way of remembering the scriptural story is not only to rely on the newest commentaries when teaching on a particular biblical text but also to explore how the passage has been understood by Christians of earlier eras. In recent decades, commentary series like the Ancient Christian Commentary on Scripture have enriched our historical understanding of biblical interpretation. Another useful resource for deepening our roots in the tradition of biblical interpretation is Thomas Aquinas's *Catena Aurea* (*Golden Chain*), which collects the wisdom of the early Christians on every passage in the four Gospels.

Remembering Our Congregation's Story

Reconnecting to and owning the story of our particular congregation can serve as a compelling means of sustaining our practices of conversation. We are not just a group of people trying to find our way in the present—although that is part of the work into which we have been called. Rather, we have a particular history that can be traced back through the centuries to the biblical people of God.

Like a tree that draws nourishment from its roots, we—and our conversations—are sustained by our historical roots, by those who have gone before us and the story they helped shape. Maintaining a congregational archive is an important part of remembering the story of our particular church. Collect and save artifacts of your congregational life: photos, newsletters, and important documents, for instance. If your church does not presently have an archive, perhaps some older members of your church have pictures and documents that could be copied and preserved as the start of an archival collection. Congregational archives do not need to be massive or elaborate. They can be as small as a drawer or plastic tote or file cabinet. Archives work best when they are not just static repositories but dynamic libraries that provide resources for the life and worship of the church. Photographs and documents, for example, can be framed as decorations for the church building (aesthetics and available space may require that these artifacts be digitally enhanced or resized). Writers in the church who are crafting songs or prayers for worship might occasionally draw on resources in the church archives. Creative preaching might also at times incorporate stories or images from the archives, telling not only of the church's faithfulness but also, carefully and gracefully, of our failures.

Making oral histories can be a fun and vital part of remembering our church's story. In almost every church there are people who would love to sit down for an hour or two and tell stories of the church in years gone by. With this person's permission, these stories can be digitally recorded. Transcription of the audio files may aid in the stories being saved and distributed: choice stories could be shared (again, with permission) in a sermon or via the church website or newsletter. Some churches have commissioned their youth to conduct oral histories, which not only ensures that stories get archived but also allows the young people to build relationships with older members of the church and perhaps recognize more fully their participation in a community that has a history.

Remembering our congregational history, of course, raises the question of how this work can be done in churches that are relatively new or in churches that consist mostly of younger people. Churches rarely spring up out of nowhere; rather, one church typically forms out of another (or through a church-planting organization), which means that even newer churches have histories they would do well to learn. Sometimes churches are created by splits, and as painful as that might be, it is worthwhile to learn and tell that story, rather than hiding it away. Recent splits may be too fresh and painful to explore, but exploring older splits may be beneficial as part of remembering our history; it may even open channels for some degree of healing and reconciliation.

Local churches are situated within particular places and can best be understood and remembered in conjunction with the stories of those places. To some degree, every church is shaped by the socioeconomic, racial, and geographic histories of its place. The demographics and economics of a place inevitably change over time, and congregations either reflect or resist these changes (sometimes even resisting to the point of relocating to a different place). In most places, there are plenty of local history resources on which to draw, and the local public library is usually a great place to start learning about the history of your place. Not only is the library a repository for some of these resources but it may also be able to connect you to local historians or history groups who have access to many more resources. In some places where local history efforts are not well organized, churches are well suited to coordinate such initiatives. About a decade ago at Englewood Christian Church, a team of our members gathered local artifacts and oral histories and published a book that told our neighborhood's story. Designed by an artist in our congregation, this book is a captivating collection not only of stories but also of maps, photographs, and other vital records of this place.

Conflicts will inevitably arise in our conversations together, as we explore in the next chapter, but we weather these storms of conflict best when we are rooted in our identity as a people who have a deep network of stories that define and sustain us. Our efforts to remember these stories—stories of Scripture, of our ancestors in the faith, of our local congregation, and of our place—not only will bind us together but also will provide the energy we need to grow and bear fruit in the present and in the years to come.

Sustaining Conversation
through Conflict

If I conclude that my Christian brother or sister is deeply and damagingly mistaken in their decision, I accept for myself the brokenness in the Body that this entails.

—Rowan Williams, "Making Moral Decisions"

Between an active childhood and several brutal accidents as an adult, I have broken at least half a dozen different bones in my body. Although I may have broken more bones than the average person, the experience of having a broken bone is something that most people will experience at some point in their lifetime. Sometimes our bodies cannot adequately coordinate themselves, and we fall and bones get fractured. In an eighth-grade soccer game, for instance, I made a slide tackle, but in doing so I threw too much weight on the hand that was breaking my fall and ended up fracturing a couple of bones in my left wrist. Other times, forces external to our bodies assault us, breaking our bones. In the summer after my freshman year of college, I was in a terrible car accident, and the force of an oncoming car broke bones in my right arm and wrist. Sometimes human bones are fractured because they are not healthy. Malnutrition or osteoporosis can lead to fractured bones that, under normal circumstances, wouldn't be broken.

When not treated properly, broken bones can affect our body's ability to move and act fluidly. Sometimes they can lead to visible deformities. In rare cases—such as some compound fractures in which broken bones pierce the skin—fractures can lead to infection and occasionally even death. Proper treatment of a broken bone begins with acknowledgment of the fracture, usually in the form of an X-ray. After the fracture is located and assessed, the bone fragments need to be set in the proper position for healing. If bones have started to heal before they are set in place, they may need to be rebroken so they can be aligned and heal properly.

Our bodies have the wondrous capacity to heal themselves, and often they recognize and begin to treat a broken bone before we even realize that it has been fractured. Through the reciprocal economy of the body, in which resources are shared with the members who need them most, the various parts of our body talk and work together to provide the resources that a fracture needs to heal. Within hours of a fracture, a blood clot takes shape around the break, and special cells called phagocytes clean the fragments of bone and kill infection and germs that might interfere with healing. The blood clot eventually turns into a callus, which will harden with time and become bone. The last phase of healing a fracture is remodeling, in which osteoclasts, a special type of cell, break down extra bone cells that surrounded the fracture, gradually molding the bone back into its original and proper shape.

In spite of the body's capacity to heal, additional care is often needed for bones to heal properly. External structures are typically added so that the bones are held in the correct position while they heal. A cast or splint is the most common sort of external structure, but in the case of extreme fractures, screws or pins might be inserted to hold the bones in the correct position. Furthermore, the healing of the body takes time and often requires diminished motion and activity so that healing is not impeded.

The care required for the healing of broken bones offers a helpful image as we reflect as churches on how to navigate conflicts in our conversations. First, many forces in the contemporary world—such as individualism, racism, partisan politics, and the widening gap between rich and poor—threaten to tear our churches apart, fracturing the very structures that give us form and enable us to move gracefully in the world. When conflicts arise, we need to acknowledge the pain we feel and assess the damage of the fracture. Next, the fracture needs to be set right—that is, we need to remember that we are diverse members of Christ's body and are committed to one another. After the fracture is set, our body may need extra support in order for the fracture to heal. We may even need to slow down for a while and to desist from certain activities in order to facilitate healing. Ultimately, healing will be found as those who are on opposing sides of the conflict are able to talk together and to remember that we are growing together into the fullness of Christ. Healing doesn't necessarily presuppose agreement, but where disagreement persists, it must be *virtuous* disagreement, in which our unity and mission in Christ supersedes the ways in which we disagree. Our ability to sustain conversations will depend in large part on our ability to navigate conflict faithfully, allowing Christ to heal the fractures and wounds that have been inflicted on our body.

Inevitability of Conflict

The modern age has been one of fragmentation: the fragmenting of empires into nation-states, the fragmenting of the one catholic church (in the West) into hundreds of varieties of Protestant denominations, the fragmenting of families and communities by individualism, the fragmenting of places by the transportation revolution, and these are only a handful of the fragmenting forces of our age. These forces slam against our churches, just as they slam against our society at large.

We must acknowledge that these fragmenting forces do not just exist "out there," in our churches, our neighborhoods, and society at large; they also exist in every one of our hearts and minds. "Tensions," writes Jean Vanier of L'Arche, "come from conflicts within each person."[1] Amid the messiness of life and the fragmenting powers of our age, we each face conflict and disorder in our own souls. We do best when we acknowledge this internal conflict and submit ourselves to the guidance of the Holy Spirit in our church communities, which binds us together and heals us.

Perhaps the most intense of the forces that threaten to tear our congregations apart is scriptural interpretation. Various members will read and interpret the same biblical passage in widely different ways, often in ways that dovetail with that member's political or socioeconomic convictions. Was the universe created in seven literal days? Or are the biblical references to seven days of creation metaphorical devices that have a nonliteral meaning? Do biblical passages prohibiting homosexual practice apply in all ages and cultural contexts? Or were they—like passages about women being silent in church—intended only for particular people in particular situations? Conflict arising from scriptural interpretation is so intense in churches because it revolves around the story at the heart of our life together, our common identity, and our embodiment of the gospel in our particular places.

As we learn to talk together, we should be careful to distinguish between disagreement and conflict. Disagreements are a natural part of human societies, of living together with other human beings. Disagreements do not necessarily precipitate conflict. Rather, conflict is disagreement that has become insidious and is ripping a community apart. We find ourselves in conflict when we layer all sorts of sin and distrust on top of our disagreements. Impatience, jealousy, bitterness, judgment, and demonization are just a few of the seeds that turn disagreement into conflict. In the stories of the earliest churches that are recorded in the biblical books of Acts and the Epistles, disagreements abound—over whether they could eat meat sacrificed to idols, for example—yet Paul and the other apostles are unwavering in their view that these disagreements must be navigated in love and compassion lest they turn sour in conflict and tear God's people apart.

Too many churches remain shallow and immature because they go to great lengths to avoid the tiniest semblance of disagreement. Authoritarian leadership—whether exercised by an individual or by a group—is one way churches attempt to avoid conversation and its tendency to reveal disagreement. Authoritarian leaders lay down the law and then seek to punish or cut off those who cannot abide by their law. This sort of leadership imposes a sharp order on a world that is not nearly so neat (recall our exploration of the prevalence of messiness in chap. 6). In criticizing authoritarian leadership, I am not seeking to abolish leadership or morality. We need standards to give shape to our common life, but how do these standards emerge? And how are those who disagree with them—whether conceptually or in practice—treated? The latter half of Matthew 18 (vv. 15–35) is often discussed as Jesus's wisdom on church discipline, but the end that Jesus is moving toward seems to be not punitive—punishing the wrongdoer—but, rather, conciliatory, being reconciled when there has been a divide.[2] Authoritarian leadership is quick to punish and exile; healthy leadership, in contrast, acknowledges disagreements, facilitates conversations about them, and holds the community together while disagreements are discerned in light of the way of Jesus, the wisdom of Scripture, and the traditions we have inherited as a particular community of God's people.

Virtuous Disagreement

In many cases, fractures in our church bodies will be healed as conflict is patiently transformed, through conversation, into virtuous disagreement. In his book *Disagreeing Virtuously*, Olli-Pekka Vainio names three specific virtues that keep communities in conversation even when they disagree: open-mindedness, humility, and courage. Open-mindedness, he writes, "entails engaging a serious thought exam: even if I hold these beliefs, I will try to inhabit a different mode of thinking that is not common to me. Second, an open-minded person engages in dialectical deliberation by reflecting the strengths and weaknesses of both his or her own and opposing position(s). Third, open-mindedness entails that we must sometimes remain in a state of uncertainty and avoid drawing hasty conclusions."[3] Vainio emphasizes that we cannot be open-minded toward everything; rather, open-mindedness is a virtue when we can reasonably expect it to lead us in the direction of truth.

The second virtue that Vainio names, and one deeply related to open-mindedness, is humility. This virtue, he asserts, is defined by a proper estimation—not over- or underestimating—of oneself and one's convictions. Humility also includes the capacity to temporarily set aside one's personal agenda, looking at things from a broader perspective. The humble person can articulate not only the weaknesses and strengths of her own convictions; she also knows the weaknesses and strengths of a differing perspective and can constructively relate the two perspectives.

Vainio's final virtue of disagreement is courage, which he defines as "a voluntary state of mind that involves conscious judgment to act in proper ways in the face of danger."[4] Following Aquinas, Vainio observes that courage is formed by the Pauline triad of virtues: faith, hope, and love. Courage is guided by the love of God and love of neighbor, not love of self or of one's own selfish agenda. Community, he observes, can also be a catalyst of courage. "Strong leadership, mutual trust, and bonding among community members," writes Vainio, "also enable courage."[5]

Acknowledging Our Fractures

The process by which our bodies heal fractured bones can be instructive for churches as we seek the healing of conflicts that are tearing our bodies apart. The first sign of a broken bone is usually pain in the area surrounding the fracture. In our churches, shame can be an intense form of pain, when people's convictions or experiences fall outside what the church deems to be normal. In various contexts, shame may be felt by those of lower incomes, those who have been divorced, those who have been physically or sexually abused, those in the LGBTQ community (or those with children or other close family members who identify as LGBTQ), and those with mental illness, among others. Pain also may be felt by those who perceive themselves to be taken as less than full participants in the life of the church due to gender, race, ethnicity, or educational status.

Our church bodies must be attentive to these sorts of pains that our members feel—especially pain related to their interactions with other church members or with the body as a whole. Untreated fractures can lead to infection that intensifies the body's pain or to the disfigurement of the body. How do we become attentive to the pain of our members, especially in large churches in which anonymity is prevalent and often preferred? The place to begin is in smaller relational units—for instance, friendships or smaller groups—where sufficient trust has been cultivated so that members are willing to talk about their pain. Given the vital importance of trust, members' experiences of pain should be handled with care. Sometimes if the pain stems from a particular person (in a nonabusive way), the one in pain should be encouraged to talk directly to that person in the manner Jesus described in Matthew 18.

Other times a broader church conversation may be necessary. Except in cases of a credible threat to someone's life or well-being, this pain should *not* be shared beyond the group—whether with leaders or with others in the church—without the explicit permission of the one who is experiencing the pain. If the person is not yet ready to have their pain shared more broadly, those who have earned that person's confidence should help to bear the burden of that pain as best they can.

Many people in our churches experience pain from our theology, our convictions about how we should live as followers of Jesus, or our particular habits of sharing life together. Churches can be toxic places, wounding and manipulating our members, but such toxicity thrives most under the veil of secrecy, when the pains of our members cannot be acknowledged and addressed in truth and love. Yes, acknowledging the pain felt among our members may compound and spread that pain, but we will not find healing while we continue to ignore the pain of our members. Our body may not be mature enough to address every pain that our members experience, but our willingness to name and bear the burden of a particular pain is far more Christlike than ignoring or covering up that pain. David Janzen, a long-time member of Reba Place Fellowship, an intentional Christian community in Evanston, Illinois, writes, "[Any] source of tension or conflict is reason to enter into dialogue with reconciling intent."[6]

Working to assess our pain includes efforts to understand its origins, whether it stems from relationships with particular people or from particular convictions or practices of the church. Honest conversation with the person or people who are feeling this pain can help us understand the exact nature of its cause (and often there are multiple factors causing or amplifying the pain) and begin to imagine structures that will pull together the members who are being torn apart, thus allowing for the healing of our body.

Aligning the Fractured Parts

Before we can implement structures that will support our body as it heals, we need to align the fractured parts. Alignment does not mean that we agree on everything but rather that we are committed to belonging to one another and to moving toward similar ends. Our alignment and the shape of our body, therefore, is found in Jesus Christ. To align ourselves is to reaffirm that it is Christ who created us and Christ who unites us in his life, death, resurrection, and ascension, and that our bonds in Christ run deeper than any disagreement we might have. Just as realigning broken bones can be very painful, aligning disagreeing factions of our church body can bring great pain, especially when the conflict has escalated to the point that one or both sides see the other as having abandoned the way of Jesus. A friend of mine recently described this alignment process as the acknowledgment of "like-heartedness." Churches often talk of like-mindedness, but perhaps, my friend argued, we should focus on like-heartedness. Do we all, for instance, desire to follow in the way of Jesus? Listening can be a vital part of the alignment process as each side hears the other explain how their position strives to be faithful to the way of Jesus. The intent of this sort of conversation is not to convert the other side but to illuminate our like-heartedness in Christ.

The process of realignment might include a profession—in a worship service, for instance—from both sides that although they disagree, they are united in their desire to follow Jesus, in their commitment to live together as Christ's body in this place, and in their desire to seek the guidance of the Holy Spirit and the healing of Christ.

We might easily be tempted to skip the alignment part of the healing process and to move from assessing our fracture to implementing structures that promote healing. The process of aligning ourselves in our common identity as followers of Jesus, however, is a powerful liturgy that will stand in our memories as a compelling reminder of Christ's body, into which we are being formed. Alignment can play a crucial role in sustaining us through the pain and impatience of the healing season. Without realignment, the structures that we imagine for supporting our body during healing may in fact form us into some shape other than that of Jesus.

Supporting the Fracture

Once we have acknowledged the pain in our body and understand exactly where the fracture lies, we can work to provide structures that promote a good and healthy healing of the fracture. Depending on the nature of the fracture, we might need internal supports (analogous to pins or screws that hold broken bones together inside the body) or external supports (analogous to a cast or splint that is applied to the outside of the body), or even both internal and external supports. Internal supports often involve a series of internal conversations that bring together those on both (or multiple) sides of a divide that is causing pain.

At other times, external structures may be necessary in order for fractures to heal. Sometimes, for instance, the body will have to cease certain activities—even good and healthy activities—in order to orient the body's energy and resources toward healing a particular fracture. During the first five years of our Sunday night conversations at Englewood Christian Church, we weren't very involved with our neighbors or with other churches. We felt the pain of not having a clear sense of who we were as a church community and of not being able to talk together very well. In this same period, we made the contentious decision to end our large-scale food, clothing, and furniture pantry ministry because it was not bringing us into deeper relationships with our neighbors.

We had to cease activities like these in order to allow some of the fractures in our body to heal. Specifically, we devoted more of our energy to learning to talk with one another in more Christlike ways and to clarifying our sense of who we were as a church and in what direction we believed God was leading us. We also devoted more energy to caring for our own members, whom we had largely neglected in previous years. Eventually, as some of the fractures in our body began to heal, we again became more active in our work with our neighbors and other churches—though our work with neighbors took on new forms (e.g., early-childhood education and affordable housing) that we hoped would prove to be healthier for our church body and our neighborhood.

Another external structure that a church might utilize in the process of addressing fractures in its body is conversation with wise Christian sisters and brothers outside that church. Some congregations may belong to denominations that have systems in place for providing this sort of counsel. Others may want to arrange their own conversations with people from local (or nonlocal) churches that are familiar with their particular situation. As we pursue these external conversations, we may face a powerful temptation to invite others in for the purpose of healing our wounds and fixing our problems. We should be ever wary of this temptation. Rather, our purpose in consulting the wisdom of other churches and followers of Christ is to draw on their broader perspective to shed light on our own situation and to clarify the work that our congregation needs to do as we seek the healing of fractures in our body. Humility is needed on the part of the church that is asking for outside wisdom and support, but it is equally necessary on the part of those outsiders who are providing counsel. Ideally, the outsiders would spend most of their time listening to the church and would offer feedback primarily in the form of observations based on what they have heard, not in the form of recommendations. In instances where recommendations are offered, these need to be discerned by the church to determine if and how they should be acted on.

Drawing on an immense well of experience in providing outside support to various church communities, David Janzen describes the spirit in which consultation should be given and received:

> I remember at the end of visitation reports we have often said something like this: "Our team feels immensely honored by your trust and honest sharing with us. We have given you our observations, commendations, and a few suggestions of possible changes. We are fallible humans trying to hear you all and listen to the Spirit. So don't take ours as the final word for what you should do. Take what we have said, discuss it, and sit with it before the Lord. See what your spirits and the Holy Spirit confirm. 'Whoever has ears, let them hear what the Spirit says to the churches.'"[7]

Healing Fractures

Before exploring the process of healing, it is important to clarify our expectations so that we can be attentive to and grateful for God's healing work. First, we must remember that a fracture in our church body can, and likely will, be healed without requiring unanimity. Yes, God has united us in Christ, but we don't yet know fully what that unity will look like. After all, the Triune God is three diverse persons who indwell one another. One of the limitations of our finite human knowledge is that we don't know the ways in which the Trinity's diversity will be reflected in the unity of Christ's body into which we are being transformed. And so we must abide in the messiness of our human condition, realizing that healing often takes the form of trust that binds us together and that enables us to work together in spite of our disagreements. Our aim therefore should not be complete unanimity but rather embodying the reconciling love of Christ that is drawing together all people from all backgrounds and perspectives.

A second important expectation that we should keep in mind during the healing process is that healing will take time, usually much more time than we wish it would. Being patient through this season of God healing our body cuts against the grain of our formation in a culture of instant gratification. To learn patience in a season of healing is to be formed into the love of Christ that is, above all, patient (1 Cor. 13:4). The patience that is needed to heal a particular fracture does not demand that the body cease all activity, just as you or I would not cease all activity if we had a broken finger. Once, when I broke a bone in my foot, the doctor put a walking cast on it and told me to take it easy. I would have to wear the cast for six weeks, he told me, but if after three weeks I didn't experience any pain in walking, I could walk as normally as possible, given the cast. I suspect that something similar is true for our churches: activity that is closely related to a fracture may have to cease temporarily while we await God's healing, but eventually if we are attentive to the pain in the area of the fracture, we may resume activity.

One final expectation is that healing will come in conversation. Just as our body parts talk and work together to heal broken bones, so too fractures in our churches cannot be healed without conversation. Too often, we would rather ignore the pain or cut it off than actually have a conversation because that might mean we would have to change. Of course, healing comes with a particular kind of conversation, one that acknowledges the fracture and that is structured to foster healing. Just as our bodies contain certain types of cells that play a crucial role in holding broken bones together and helping them heal, our congregations will contain peacemakers who hold our fractured parts together and keep them talking and working toward healing.

A Congregation Being Healed

Grandview Calvary Baptist Church is a congregation of about three hundred members that is very active in its neighborhood on the east side of Vancouver, British Columbia. They are part of the Canadian Baptist denomination, which maintains a traditionalist understanding of sexuality and doesn't allow member churches to marry same-sex couples or to ordain pastors who are in same-sex marriages. Grandview's denominational heritage combined with a thriving LGBTQ community in their urban neighborhood have led to fractures in their body related to questions about same-sex relationships. Their church has spent recent years addressing these fractures in conversation and discernment, allowing God to heal their wounds.

The fractures in Grandview's life together, for instance, were identified over the course of a decade in the pain and confusion of same-sex couples who regularly visited their church but didn't know where they stood with the congregation. Could they become members? Could their gifts be utilized in the life of the church? Or were they relegated to the margins of the congregation? These pains and the fractured convictions about sexuality that precipitated them initiated a yearlong process of exploration that included preaching and teaching aimed at opening up conversation among the church body.

The yearlong process of exploration at Grandview culminated with a statement of common ground in matters of human sexuality on which the church could all agree. (This statement is included as appendix C at the end of this book.) This statement begins with the affirmation that all humans are created in the image of God; it goes on to recognize the complex origins of any sexual desire and concludes with the affirmation that the church's convictions and practices about sexuality "are important, but not part of the essential teachings of the church." This statement served to align the congregation in such a way that God could heal the fractures related to sexuality in their body.

Grandview experienced immense pain due to varying convictions about same-sex relationships in their church. After working diligently to understand the exact points of disagreement that were causing pain, they initially adopted a compromise that would support the healing of the fracture. This compromise sought to build on the common ground around which they were aligned, to recognize their disagreements, to welcome both gay and straight people into membership and allow all members to use their gifts in the life of the church, and to serve in leadership, with the exception of pastoral and church council positions (which allowed their congregation to remain in fellowship with their denomination and thus also to retain their building and presence in their neighborhood).

This arrangement would later be challenged by another fracture; a situation arose that challenged the church to clarify its stance on sexuality. Conflict was intense for Grandview in the weeks that followed. Not only was the congregation still divided in its members' perspectives on sexuality—from traditionalists to those who affirmed same-sex marriages—but Grandview was also divided on how their church should engage their denomination on these questions. Some people in the church felt that the congregation should stand with their gay and lesbian brothers and sisters and against their denomination. Others knew that to do so would be to put their church building and their long-established presence in the Grandview neighborhood at risk. Along with the conflict came a deep sense of being stuck, of neither side being able to convince the other to change their minds. The crucial question that emerged in this season was, How do we love one another in this intractable situation? The congregation may not agree with one another, one leader observed, but perhaps they could go deeper in their love and understanding of one another.

With this hope in mind, the church decided to send a representative group of their members on a retreat that they referred to as a "deeper dialogue." They selected twelve members whom they recognized as spiritually mature, ones whose priority was moving toward Christ (and not the advancement of their own personal perspective). These twelve were selected because, in addition to the spiritual maturity they possessed, they represented a wide range of perspectives on sexuality, as well as a diverse mix of genders, ages, and experiences. Before the retreat, each participant was asked to reflect in writing on a short list of questions in order to come prepared with thoughts to discuss at the retreat. One of the church's pastors also met with each participant before the date of the retreat. She recalls that there was fear and apprehension on all sides of the disputed questions on sexuality.

As the retreat got under way, the group was reminded of the central question: How do we love one another well, even when we vehemently disagree? They also began with a reflection on Philippians 2, reminding themselves that their shared hope was to grow in the mind and humility of Christ. Most of the retreat was spent in telling and listening to one another's stories about how their views on sexuality had been formed, in grappling with the witness of Scripture, and in talking about other experiences and relationships that may have shaped the perspectives of each participant. Times of conversation among the whole group were punctuated with smaller group conversations that allowed each person to share in greater detail. When they reconvened as a large group, each small group would summarize its conversation.

The retreat ended with a time of sharing among participants of what they had learned over the course of the retreat. It was during this time that the movement of the Holy Spirit became most apparent. The pervasive fear and anxiety that the group brought into the retreat had dissipated. "We may disagree," said one participant, "but I can go into our church meetings and know that you all have my back." The group agreed that this retreat was a powerful experience of talking openly with one another and learning to do the hard work of loving one another. As the group came back and eventually shared stories of their experience with the church, they bore witness to the possibility of a different way of loving one another and being Christ's body together. This retreat is a good example of an internal structure that aligned the members of the body and oriented them all toward healing and wholeness.

Although churches like Grandview and Englewood are finding some degree of healing as we doggedly commit to staying in conversation and to learning to disagree virtuously, our bodies are much bigger than our disagreements. We share life together daily, working to bear witness to the very good news of Jesus in varied ways among our neighbors. We will explore this rich, interconnected community life in the next chapter, as it serves to provide ample things for us to talk about and helps keep us from becoming unhealthfully obsessed with our brokenness. In short, this rich, interwoven community life is essential to sustaining conversations in our churches.

10

Enmeshing Ourselves in the Dance of Community

> Let us whirl round in the waltz's gay measure.
>
> —Goethe, "Reciprocal Invitation to the Dance"

In elementary school, gym class was by far my favorite. I loved to play sports, but there was one unit in gym class that I was never excited about. As an introverted and slightly less than coordinated boy, I always dreaded the time each year when we would square dance in gym. I worried that my lack of rhythm and coordination, along with my preteen awkwardness with girls, would result in certain humiliation. What I didn't realize at the time was that most of my classmates were similarly awkward, and we all bumbled our way through the square dancing unit each year without anyone being traumatically humiliated.

As a young seminary student, Eugene Peterson had a similar uncomfortable experience with square dancing:

[Peterson] wasn't a particularly good or confident dancer, so he'd usually start on the sidelines. He'd watch folks as they danced, seeing partners swap, join hands, circle up. But as the dance got faster and faster—as it does—the individuals became almost indistinguishable, a blur of movement and motion. And, he said, at some point a hand would reach out and he'd get yanked in—all of a sudden part of the dancing. He was dancing not because he was particularly good at it, but because he was with those who knew how to dance.[1]

Peterson went on to suggest that the life of the Triune God was similar. However uncomfortable we might be at first, we are invited into this dance of abundant life, and we learn its rhythms and its steps as we go along. Before we know it, we are whirling around our place in beautiful and intricate ways with our sisters and brothers in Christ and with our neighbors. The practice of conversation, as I have described it in this book, although vital to the life and well-being of our communities, is never the primary thing for churches. In conversation, we learn the graceful maneuvers of life with others in the presence of God. We learn how to listen, how to speak the truth courageously, how to imagine next steps together, how to forgive those who have wounded us and be reconciled. Interweaving all these virtuous skills and more, conversation is a means to an end: action—namely, the graceful dance of our communal body on the stage of our place. We practice conversation together in order to sync our body better with the mind of Christ and to coordinate and train ourselves to move with the beauty and compassion of Christ among our neighbors.

Our action together, however, also has a symbiotic relationship with our conversations. The more we work together as a body, the more we have to discuss and discern in conversation. If we restrict our conversations to the narrow scope of our life as a religious community (that is, abstract conversations about the theological and practical issues limited to the shape of our liturgy and worship), we will find that they will be nearly impossible to sustain. Rather, if our conversations are interwoven with a robust life in which our community acts together in a multitude of diverse ways, caring for one another and for our neighbors, celebrating and grieving together, working toward the flourishing of our place and bearing witness in substantial ways to God's reconciliation of *all* things (Col. 1:20), we will find that we can't stop talking together.

Our churches will best be able to sustain conversation when we are not merely religious communities but *real* communities that enter into the fullness of life together. The two crucial distinctions between a religious community and a real community are time and place. While a real community exists and shares life throughout the days and weeks, a religious community exists only during specific windows of time when it gathers for worship or other religious activities. Similarly, a real community exists within a particular place and is interwoven with the life of that place. In contrast, a religious community exists apart from its physical location; its members may commute in from other places, and its people are largely unknown by neighbors in the vicinity of the church building.

Another crucial difference between real and religious communities is the scope of their economy. The economy of a religious community is largely focused on growing its membership, sustaining its institution, paying its staff, maintaining its facilities, and keeping its utilities running. The economy of a real community is much broader, encompassing all the resources of its members and concerned with their flourishing. Real communities are intimately engaged in the health, housing, education, employment, diets, and recreation of their members. Indeed, a real community is comprehensive; there is nothing in the life of its members and neighbors that exists outside the scope of its concern. To the extent that it exists comprehensively as a real community, a local church has the opportunity to bear witness to the "manifold wisdom of God"

(Eph. 3:9 NASB) that is reconciling *all* things in Christ Jesus. A real community that is comprehensive in scope has much more to talk about, and a much broader arena within which it must discern and act, than a religious community. Most churches, of course, exist somewhere on the spectrum between a religious community and a real community. If a phrase like "churches don't do that" (or "can't do that") is a common refrain in your conversations, you are probably closer to the religious community end of the spectrum.

For the past three decades, the church to which I belong, Englewood Christian Church, has been on the journey from being a religious community toward being a real community. In the early years, we heard "churches don't do that sort of thing" a lot, but eventually and with much conversation, we did many of the things that we once thought were forbidden to churches—buying and selling property, starting businesses, partnering with government agencies and the United Way, educating children, helping local businesses to launch and grow, as a few examples. Our journey in this direction began when we had shrunk to our smallest size as a congregation. We discovered that some of our older women were in bad housing arrangements, and we worked to fix up the houses near the church building where they could live affordably and be looked after by people in the church.

Around the same time that we were beginning to care for some of the seniors in our church body, we also began a co-op preschool, in which mothers got together a few mornings a week to do activities with their young children. In the mid-1990s, when the federal government was pushing mothers on welfare to go to work, this co-op was expanded into a daycare that served not only our children but also those of our neighbors. This daycare has grown and expanded during the past two decades and now has over two hundred children enrolled, from birth to prekindergarten.

Three decades ago, when our church was at its smallest, over three-quarters of our congregation drove to church activities from the suburbs or other parts of the city, and only one-quarter lived in this neighborhood. Today, these numbers have flip-flopped, with more than three-quarters of our church members living in our neighborhood and one-quarter driving from other places. We haven't had a program aimed at getting people to move into the neighborhood, nor have we twisted people's arms to move here. Rather, our neighborhood presence has grown in three ways. First, the largest growth has come from families like mine, who see the life and activity that flows in and around the church building and want to move to be enfolded into this life. Second, we have had a number of young people who have grown up in our church and, after going away to college, eventually choose to settle in our neighborhood and devote themselves to the life of the church here. Third, neighbors who already live in the neighborhood are intrigued enough by the church to want to join us. Sometimes these neighbors live in homes that we own; other times their children are enrolled in our daycare, or they meet us through neighborhood work in which we are engaged. With so many people in close proximity, we have all kinds of formal and informal activities going on. People share meals together in a variety of ways. Some people work together, not only in businesses that we own but also informally in gardens and in the various tasks involved in caring for this place. We not only work together but also play together—in sports leagues, in our youth running club, and in a long list of neighborhood festivities that span the calendar.

The church members who live in our neighborhood are a diverse lot, from the older folks living in our recently opened senior housing development to the youth whose families live here or who have recently graduated from school and moved into their own house or apartment. All the life and activity of this place give us time to be and to talk together, and they give us much to talk about. We eventually circle around to questions of what it means to do this work (or this recreational activity) in the way of Jesus. Our journey during the past three decades has taken us from being primarily a religious community to one that is more fully a real community. I will use some stories from our church community throughout this chapter to highlight the role of a vibrant, multi-sided community life in sustaining practices of conversation.

The Fragmentation of Our Days

In the early twenty-first century, we live amid widespread fragmentation, not only political fragmentation (which endlessly fuels the news media) but also fragmentation of our neighborhoods, families, schools, neighborhoods, and even fragmentation from the land and the food it provides to sustain us. One of the deepest and most ubiquitous divides that faces most adults in North America is the fragmentation of our days—and indeed our lives—into the distinct spheres of home, work, church, and in some instances school. Each of these spheres has its own community of people, and very little overlaps among the people and the activities of each sphere. We end up having to devote significant portions of our time, energy, and anxiety to meeting and exceeding the expectations of each sphere. Much of the anxiety stems from the demands of multiple spheres coming into conflict. Our workplaces, for instance, often have little overlap with our home lives, and with minimal overlap comes little knowledge or incentive for collaboration for the good of both spheres. For all the talk of "work-life balance" in the business world, most employers offer little flexibility in difficult situations, for instance, when a family member needs daily care over the long term.

This fragmentation of our days also manifests itself in the alarming amount of time and energy we use in commuting between spheres: home and work, home and church, and so on. The twentieth century was the age of the automobile, and the increasing prevalence of cars and highways made it possible to live farther and farther away from our work and church communities, and it served to widen the gap between these spheres. If I were to plot all my travels over the course of a normal week, we could see that my travels range much farther than the travels of my grandparents or great-grandparents ever did and that the radius of the circle encompassing my travels is substantially—and in some cases exponentially—larger. This distance not only makes it less likely that the spheres of our church members' lives will overlap and allow for meaningful collaboration; it also means that our travel between spheres erodes a portion of the time we could spend being present and working in a given sphere.

Automobility, along with the acceleration of other travel technologies during the past century, has been a key factor in the fragmentation of our days. More expedient forms of travel have not only expanded the geography of our daily lives; they have also made it increasingly tempting to go away to colleges that are far removed from the places in which we were born and raised and in this way have contributed on a broader scale to the hypermobility of society. An alarming percentage of adults in the United States have moved to a completely new place (not just to a new home in the same place) within the last five years. This hypermobility inhibits the spiritual and relational growth that comes from the stability of journeying with the same group of people—at work or at church—over a long stretch of time. Hypermobility also makes it difficult for extended families to care for one another through the challenges of illness or aging.

Another factor that has contributed to the fragmentation of our days is the expanding scope of businesses in a global economy. Companies are no longer selling goods or providing services solely in one particular place; they are expanding their markets across state and national boundaries. Companies are often bought out by larger companies, and buyouts usually shuffle employees to new places or new roles. Businesses with national or international markets require some employees who can manage operations in multiple places, often at the cost of frequent time away from home. The forces of business expansion also widen the gap between the spheres of our lives.

Homogenization is yet another force contributing to the fragmentation of our days. Journalist Bill Bishop, you'll recall from the introduction, calls this force "the big sort"—that is, the increasing desire during the past half century to live, work, and worship with people who are of similar economic, ethnic, racial, and ideological backgrounds. The accelerating fragmentation of the spheres of our lives is a price we pay in order to live in homogeneous neighborhoods and worship in homogeneous churches. We will live farther away from our churches and workplaces in order to be in a homogeneous community where we fit in. And considering the pace at which our hypermobile culture moves, places are not inclined to stay homogeneous for the long haul—so if we want to live in homogeneous communities, we will often have to move to new places as the ones we are in begin to diversify.

Homogenization has been at work in the history of North American suburbs since World War II, driving families out of cities and then farther and farther from the urban core as ethnic and economic diversity spread into the suburbs. I suspect that the desire for homogeneous communities is often an expression of our longing for some semblance of familiarity and stability in a fragmenting and rapidly shifting world. The irony, of course, is that these desires likely do *more* to destabilize us and to accelerate fragmentation by widening the scope of the spheres of our daily life.

The fragmentation of our daily lives into the spheres of home, work, and church also inhibits our capacity for conversation. Each sphere has its own language, specialized terms and phrases that fit the work to be done in that sphere. The greater the fragmentation between spheres, the more we will struggle to communicate well in one or more of the spheres—all too often the sphere that ends up suffering most in this regard is the church, since the spheres of home and work tend to culturally take priority for most people. It is little wonder then that when we bring the members of our churches together for conversation—members who work diligently to be successful at home and at work—they have little capacity to talk about their faith and their life together in the church. Most members who have been committed to the Christian faith for large portions of their lives will have theological convictions that formed along the way but will lack any real sense of how these convictions developed historically or how they might be distinguished from convictions held by those in other streams of the Christian tradition. In our hypermobile world, many of our church's members and attendees likely did not grow up in our congregation or even in our denomination or historical tradition, which means we have wide-ranging theological convictions and language that we may not even recognize. And typically we don't have the energy or imagination to sort through this diversity of perspectives.

Certainly this situation is the one that we found ourselves in as our church began Sunday night conversations over two decades ago. We rapidly came to realize the diversity of our convictions and even the varied meanings that we gave to shared terms like "gospel" and "salvation" and "the kingdom of God." Having little sense of how to hold on and work through this diversity, our early conversations were extraordinarily volatile as we tried to convert one another to our own particular understandings. For almost a decade, our Sunday evening conversations were devoted to working through these convictions and learning to trust one another in spite of our differing convictions and terminologies. Today we still often struggle with differing convictions, but the regular practice of conversation, together with a rich community life in which the spheres of our lives are gradually starting to overlap, give us hope that God will continue to transform us.

Toward the Overlapping of Our Daily Spheres

Once we are convinced that the growing divide between the spheres of our daily lives erodes our well-being and capacity for conversation, how do we begin to move in a different direction? Even before we begin to move, we need to recognize how deeply these spheres have been ingrained in us and try not to be too idealistic about the degree to which they can be integrated. Toward what end should we move? The goal, I believe, should *not* be for the spheres to coincide completely, as that would create a largely insular community that has few bonds with neighbors and the outside world. Rather, our hope should be to begin to see *some* overlap among the spheres. As I argued above, automobility is a key force that pulls the spheres of our lives apart; therefore, creating a meaningful sense of proximity in our congregations can be a vital force that pulls the spheres in the opposite direction—toward one another.

The virtues of proximity have become of increasing interest to Christian leaders in recent years, and many books have been written that explore these virtues.[2] I won't, therefore, try to recommend a detailed plan of how to cultivate proximity, but I will offer a few suggestions. When trying to cultivate proximity, perhaps the first place to start is the simple task of mapping where your church's members live and work. Theologian Willie Jennings has noted that in the twenty-first century most organizations—from global corporations to nonprofits like the Girls Scouts—map where their customers and members live. Why, he asks, don't churches do this?[3] In most medium or large churches, mapping will reveal some surprises: a church member who lives a block away or another who works around the corner from our house. After doing the mapping, encourage members in close proximity to get to know one another and to explore what it means to be an expression of God's people in the place where they are—for example, sharing meals with one another and with neighbors or doing social or recreational activities together.

Proximity has become a crucial aspect of life together at our church, but we have cultivated it slowly over more than two decades. Having the luxury of a low-cost housing market here in

Indianapolis and working on housing in our neighborhood have certainly worked to our advantage (if someone wants to live in the Englewood neighborhood where the church is, we can help them do that). Being involved in a wide range of activities in the church and in the neighborhood makes it attractive for some church members to move into the neighborhood or for young people coming out of college to settle here. We also have the benefit of our church having been here for well over a century, so our identity has long been intertwined with that of our neighborhood. Our proximity allows us to interact daily with our brothers and sisters, caring for one another in our struggles, celebrating our joys together. Sometimes our interactions are planned; other times they are spontaneous—for instance, brief conversations in passing. Our proximity draws the spheres of our daily lives closer to one another.

Beyond mapping and encouraging our members to be more engaged with one another, we should ask, What kind of work can we do together? This work might be an expression of care for our neighbors or our place, or it might generate some income, or perhaps some of both. It might take the form of immersing ourselves in local youth sports programs (coaching, refereeing, groundskeeping, or selling concessions) or in crafting a high-quality product that members or neighbors will want to buy—freshly baked bread or locally roasted coffee, for example.

Regardless of the scale on which it is done—from a handful of hours each month to daily work that employs many people—there are thousands if not millions of possibilities of what churches could do together. Start small, with things that people are gifted to do and that they can get excited about. Having fun doing this work together not only takes the dread out of working but also makes it attractive for others to want to join in and stick with it. Look for ways to include children and youth in this work. Working alongside adults in meaningful endeavors is an important way to teach our children what it means to belong to a community and to shape their desires to want to be committed to a community of God's people for life. Engaging children and youth in the work of the church is essential to bringing the spheres of home and church closer together. From visiting sick members of our congregation to cleaning our church building to working in our community gardens, we have tried to include the children of Englewood Christian Church in the work we do.

Ultimately, the work of bringing the spheres of our lives closer together requires imagination. The fundamental question has to do with how we can participate in our home or work life in a way that is more deeply connected with our church life and with the members of our church community. Although asking this question may take us out of our comfort zones, the answers do not have to be burdensome, especially when we ask what things we are already doing at home or work that could be done with others from our church. Are you going out to eat? Invite others from your church to come along. Are your kids in youth sports? Sign them up in leagues with other children from church. Do your work responsibilities include hiring employees? Hire qualified people from your church when possible. Do you have members of your church who live within close walking distance? Are there tools or other things you can share, such as a lawn mower, an extension ladder, or a garden tiller? Can you coordinate transporting children to school with others from your church or workplace?

Moving toward a more integrated life will not be without its challenges though. Every challenge will present us with a real situation in which we can practice conversation. What do you do when sharing a lawn mower and one person always returns it with an empty gas tank? Or what about when you hire people from church, but they aren't doing the work well? Or when someone in your carpool is consistently late in getting the kids to school? All of these awkward situations beg for conversation. Granted, conversation may not resolve these situations, but if the issue and conversation about it persists, we just might come to know that other person—and his or her struggles—a bit better. Having difficult conversations like these about the daily stuff of our lives will also prepare us to work through difficult conversations in our churches.

Orchestrating Our Vocations[4]

Another key for our churches in bringing the daily spheres of life closer together and in fostering a more robust community life, is the work of learning to orchestrate the vocations of all the members of our church community. Just as there are no extraneous parts in our human bodies, there are no extraneous members in our churches. If our church body is to be healthy, each person will have a function, a role to play in the sensing, discerning, and moving of our body. The challenge, of course, is imagining a way of life in which *every* person's gifts and skills can be meaningfully engaged in the life and work of the church community.

In recent years, many excellent books on vocation have emerged that challenge us to think theologically about vocation. While these books call us to a deeper integration of our faith and our work, few if any have much imagination for the role the local church plays in discerning, maturing, and orchestrating the vocations of its members. What exactly are the gifts that God has given us for the strengthening and maturing of our body as we grow into the fullness of Christ (Eph. 4)? Often churches answer this question too narrowly, focusing on the work of pastors, teachers, musicians, and administrators to the exclusion of other gifts. To begin to orchestrate all our members into the dance of Christ's body in this place, we need to imagine our life together as bigger than the worship service, as overflowing our church building into our neighborhood. We need a vibrant life together that can meaningfully draw on the gifts of the accountant, the artist, the lawyer, the restauranteur, the teacher, the plumber, the sociology professor, the garbage man, the biologist, and even those who struggle to maintain a job or who, for whatever reason, are unable to be employed.

At Englewood Christian Church, we have three primary ways in which we orchestrate the gifts and skills of our members. First, we have started a number of different businesses, each of which draws on the gifts of members in our church and does needed work in our neighborhood (or in our relationships with other churches). We have an early-learning center that teaches and cares for young children from birth to prekindergarten. It employs over fifty people in various teaching, administrative, and service roles. We have a nonprofit community development corporation (CDC) that does affordable housing, property management, and economic development in our neighborhood. This organization is also an umbrella entity for several other businesses we have started, including a bookkeeping and a landscaping operation. The *Englewood Review of Books*, of which I am the editor, is yet another business under our CDC, and it aims to recommend a wide range of books that would be beneficial for churches to read and discuss. In total, Englewood Community Development Corporation employs about twenty people in full- or part-time roles.

A second way we seek to orchestrate the skills of our members is through official and unofficial partnerships with organizations where our members are employed. Many of these organizations are based in our neighborhood. We have a doctor who works at the health clinic not far from our church building and several people who work at the local neighborhood center that our CDC regularly collaborates with. We have members who serve in local schools: teaching, administering, and serving on boards. They do this work as members of our church, caring for the children of our neighborhood and working to help the students, their families, and the neighborhood flourish. Having members who work for neighborhood organizations facilitates partnerships between the church and these organizations, all working together for the health and well-being of this place.

Members who don't work for our businesses or at partner organizations but make their skills available for the work of the church represent a third way that we endeavor to orchestrate the gifts and skills that God has provided us as a church community. For example, one of our members is a landscaper who will occasionally do work around the church building or around properties that the CDC owns. Sometimes he does this work for free, as an expression of love. Other times he is paid a fair wage for his work, as an expression of our love for him and our respect for the skills he has. A dentist in our congregation will sometimes provide his labor on a sliding scale for members who don't have insurance or can't afford dental work. Our community gardens are maintained by a group of people who aren't paid to do this work but who love to work in the garden, especially when they're able to work as a group, which allows them to talk together as they work.

Just as different traditions of dance have emerged in cultures around the globe—arising from the diversity of people, music, and instruments—so too the dance of community will look different in your congregation than it does in mine. The pressing question is, How do we orchestrate the gifts and skills that God has provided in our community to bear witness to God's love and reconciling work to our neighbors? This question, of course, will immerse us in a sea of conversations as we seek to discover the shape of our life together. However, it will also open for us a wealth of opportunities to talk together as we live out this dance together in the years to come. Not only is this dance healthy for us, providing a multitude of opportunities to practice conversations and guiding us into a life where the spheres of daily living are more integrated; this dance, in all its joy, beauty, and energy, will also be inviting to our neighbors. The Triune God is an eternal dance, and we are invited into this dance that is the life God intends for creation.

Conclusion

Conversational Bodies Bearing Witness

Your religion is your witness is the shape your love takes.

—David Dark, *Life's Too Short
to Pretend You're Not Religious*

My body is a tangible record of my experiences, my convictions, and the histories I embody. The stiff motions of my left thumb, for instance, are a record of an accident a decade ago in which I fell off a ladder and landed on that hand. Similarly, the various scars I bear are records of other accidents that have left their marks on my body. My haircut and my beard (or lack thereof) are records of my present convictions and choices about fashion and identity. My body also reveals—to a certain extent—my own convictions about diet and exercise. Certain muscle groups at various times in my life have been more or less toned, depending on the sports I played or the training to which I committed myself.

My body is also a record of the histories that have shaped me. Most obviously, it is a record of the genetic histories of my parents and their ancestors. My height, sex, face shape, hair color, skin color, and eye color are facets of my body largely determined by genetics (though some of these facets, like hair color, can be manipulated if I desire). In a more subtle manner, my body is a record of the socioeconomic history into which I was born. The degree to which I have had access to health and dental care and the sorts of care that have been provided may likely be reflected in my body. As a child, for instance, I had a large overbite that was corrected during my teenage years with braces and other orthodontic tools. I might still have that over-bite today if my parents hadn't had the resources to pay for this orthodontic work.

Our bodies were created to bear witness. Some facets of the witness that our bodies bear are within our control. Others—such as genetics and the class and place into which we are born—cannot be controlled. "As much as I'd prefer otherwise," writes religion professor and pop-culture philosopher David Dark, "there is no on-and-off switch when it comes to my witness. It's simply the evidence of my output. My witness is the sum of everything I do and leave undone. The words are there, but the actions speak louder. Our witness isn't what we say we believe or even what we think we believe. . . . It's what we do, what we give, what we take and what we actually bring to our little worlds."[1] Our bodies, I maintain, are the epicenter of this witness.

The social bodies to which we belong—our churches, families, neighborhoods, workplaces, schools, sports teams, and more—also serve to bear witness. The shape of a social body—the ways it embraces certain people and activities but resists others—is one facet of its witness. Social bodies similarly bear witness to experiences, convictions, and histories. A church that experiences a mass exodus of members, as my own church did in the late 1970s and 1980s, will bear witness to this experience. A church that serves its neighbors in love and compassion will bear witness to the love and compassion of Christ, who leads that congregation.

Churches also bear witness to the histories from which we have emerged, including the histories of the places in which we have gathered. A church that moves from one place to another, for example, will become more accessible to the people in its new location and less accessible to people in and around its previous location. This accessibility will, over time, give shape to the congregation as members join or leave the church and become more or less involved in its life together. The aging of members functions in a similar manner, as older members may become less involved in the activities of the church while younger ones become more involved. All these factors, which give shape to our choices and actions as a church, are woven together into the witness that our church body bears in the world.

I have argued in this book that churches should acquire practices of conversation—intentional spaces of learning to listen and talk in the compassionate way of Jesus. Our practices of talking together will make possible a multitude of formal and informal conversations that guide our congregations toward health and maturity in Christ. Although God desires that our churches be healthy and mature, God is up to something bigger in the world—namely the reconciliation of all things (Col. 1:20). In learning to converse with the patient love of the Triune God, our church bodies bear witness to other social bodies of the abundant, conversational life of the Trinity into which all humankind is invited.

Our learning to listen and talk together in our churches will form us to be attentive to the possibilities for dialogue in our homes, our neighborhoods, our workplaces, and other social groups in which we are involved. As we mature in the practice of conversation, we will undoubtedly learn to work through conflicts among our members instead of continually avoiding them or lashing out in hostility. We may seek opportunities to help a particular group in the neighborhood or workplace to imagine a compelling future for itself and to align itself to move into that future. (We might even use the conversational method of Appreciative

Inquiry, introduced in chap. 4, to do so.) We might be inspired to encourage public conversations in our neighborhood, in which all neighbors would be invited to explore an opportunity or an issue facing us and to speak their convictions about how we could respond together in this particular situation. We might also be inspired to create opportunities for neighbors to talk informally together. We might invite neighbors to eat a meal in our homes or in our church building, even perhaps neighbors who would not likely choose to share a meal together.

The churches of small town Silverton, Oregon, for instance, collaborate to host a weekly dinner that anyone in the town is welcome to attend. People of various denominations, faiths, and even no faith at all gather around tables and eat and talk together. This weekly meal has been a huge success, and neighbors look forward to the meal each week. Silverton is a thriving community in part because its residents have a space in which they can listen and talk together and, breaking down the walls of fear and anxiety that divide them, come to know one another and work toward the flourishing of their place.

In Englewood, my urban neighborhood on the Near Eastside of Indianapolis, many exciting things have happened during the past decade as neighbors are increasingly talking and working with one another. In 2007, Englewood and the other neighborhoods that comprise the Near Eastside were identified as a redevelopment zone, and the city government was poised to unleash a wave of funding here. The neighborhood recognized that this funding could trigger rapid gentrification and drive out some of our more vulnerable neighbors. A coalition of neighborhood groups that included Englewood Christian Church decided to gather residents for a crucial conversation on the future of this place. We worked to pull together as large and as diverse a group as possible, providing childcare and translators for those whose participation might have been impeded by these concerns. This group of over three hundred neighbors talked together over six months in order to flesh out a plan for our neighborhood that would allow resources to flow into our place in certain areas like education, public safety, business development, and affordable housing, among others. Funding in these areas would dramatically benefit our place, but it also would serve to decelerate rather than accelerate virulent forms of gentrification.

At the outset of these neighborhood conversations, Englewood Christian Church had been practicing conversation together on Sunday nights for the better part of a decade and was well situated to help with the work of leading and cultivating this dialogue. We encouraged as many of our members as possible to participate, and they did turn out well, but many of them also did vital work like childcare and serving food that enabled robust participation from other neighbors outside our congregation. In the intervening years since these initial discussions, our neighborhood has continued to talk and work together as we have begun to implement our plan. The dynamics of our conversations have changed over time as some participants and groups have stepped out of the discussion and others have stepped in to take their place, but our discussions move forward. We assess our progress, imagine the next steps that we will need to take in each season in which we find ourselves, and then seek to bring the things we envision to life.

Englewood Christian Church continues to be one neighborhood group on the Near Eastside that is committed to conversation and the action that ensues as this place grows and matures. We also regularly seek opportunities to have meaningful conversations with other churches (locally, nationally, and around the globe), with people who are served by the work we do in early-childhood education and affordable housing, with local and state governments, and with groups who do similar work in other parts of the city and the state, among others. Conversations about food justice led our neighborhood to open the city's first food co-op, and our church dove headfirst into this discussion and work. More recently, neighborhood conversations about education have led a group of neighbors to take responsibility for administering a local public elementary school. Englewood Christian Church jumped into these discussions and has played a vital role in this ongoing work.

When churches talk about bearing witness to the conversational life of God, we may face a temptation to resist initiating or participating in discussions that are broader than our congregation because we have a deep sense of our own immaturity in talking together. While it is dangerous to rush past the practice of congregational conversations, as we run headlong into bigger and broader conversations, it is equally dangerous to avoid broader discussions altogether. We may need a season of learning how to listen and talk with one another in our churches. Depending on how frequently we are able to practice conversation, this season may last for a year, possibly two, but once this season is over, our congregational conversations should coexist alongside broader dialogues with our neighbors, with sister churches, and with others. We will continually need to grow and mature in our church conversations, but at the same time we also will need to be immersed in larger discussions that bear witness to other social bodies to the conversational life we find in the Trinity.

Not all of our members are able to participate in all our broader discussions. In some situations, we may even find we have only one member working to catalyze conversations in a particular workplace or social group. (We have seen great benefits, however, from more than one person being involved in a particular external conversation.) The members who do this work should be encouraged to see themselves doing it as an extension of our church body, a hand perhaps reaching out lovingly to touch another (social) body. In this way, not only may the member or members involved seek to act in these external conversations out of the convictions that energize the church, but they may also seek the involvement of their church body in terms of prayer, wisdom, and perhaps even resources that the church could provide (e.g., a meeting space in the church building or food to energize and encourage the participants in the gathering, to name just two among the broad range of possibilities).

Throughout the scriptural story, it seems that God's radical transformation of our broken world begins humbly in one person's encounter with the presence of God or the presence of another human. Abram encountered God's presence while he was without children, and that encounter was the seed that blossomed into the Israelite people and eventually into the broader people of God in which Jews and gentiles were united. Similarly, the Spirit-catalyzed encounter of Peter and Cornelius (Acts 10), which on the surface was a brief and humble meeting of two men and a few of their companions, would resonate through two millennia of church history. This simple first-century encounter made possible the diverse people of God—Jews and gentiles together—as we know it today.

In a similar manner, I am hopeful that the simple encounters we have as we practice conversation with the sisters and brothers of our local churches will have transformative effects that ripple through the culture of our places, our economies, our nations, and our world. The conversational bodies of our churches cannot help but bear witness to the abundant life of the Triune God. The transformation that God intends—as the above scriptural stories remind us—will be slow and will be rooted in our encounters with the presence of God and the presence of particular human beings whom God ordains to cross our paths. The continuing discernment precipitated by these encounters, our wrestling with how we live faithfully in their wake, will be the hushed voice of the Spirit guiding us step-by-step, encounter-by-encounter into the ever-transforming conversation that we call the Trinity.

Knowing and being known, learning to be mutually present with one another, sharing resources freely to the benefit of the body and those we encounter, learning to commit ourselves to life together with a diversity of others—this is the radiant life to which God calls us and all creation, into the very life of the

Trinity. This life is the end for which we were created, and toward which all creation cannot help but flow. It is life abundant. It is joy. It is our home.

May our human bodies—both personal and social—bear witness to this conversational truth that lies at the heart of our being and our becoming.

Acknowledgments

Jeni, thanks for all your support while I have been working on this book and for bearing with me as I am still learning to communicate better. I'm delighted that you're my partner on this journey, and I'm grateful for the ways you care for me and the kids.

Alex, Miriam, and Noah, thank you for your patience as I have been completing this book. I look forward to being more involved in your school activities now that I'm done.

This book would not have been possible without the Englewood Christian Church community, in which I am learning what it means to belong to a conversational body. Thanks especially to Mike Bowling and Jim Aldrich for constantly recommending resources and challenging me to reflect in deeper ways on the practice of conversation. Thanks also to Katy Lines and Susan Adams for reading every last word of this manuscript and for helping to clarify and refine my writing. Thanks to Englewood Community Development Corporation for creating space for me to share my love of books, to write books like this one, and to share our stories with churches near and far.

I am also deeply indebted to the other church communities across North America who have welcomed me as a curious visitor and shared their practices of conversation with me. These churches include Grandview Calvary Baptist Church (Vancouver, BC), Silverton Friends Church (Silverton, OR), Church of the Servant King (Eugene, OR, and Portland, OR), Springwater Community (Portland, OR), and Phinney Ridge Lutheran Church (Seattle, WA). Many other churches shared stories of their practices of conversation with me. This book is much richer for the experience and wisdom of all these churches, and I pray that God continues to lead all of them deeper into conversational life.

Thanks to all my friends who read portions of early drafts of this book and offered thoughtful feedback, including Deb Leiter, Ragan Sutterfield, David Bunker, Laura Fabrycky, Dorothy Greco, Tommy Moehlman, Jonathan Melton, Lori Wilson, Rich Jones, among others (and I apologize because I know there are other people who should be named here).

A special thanks to John Pattison, whose collaboration with me on the *Slow Church* book provided the ecclesiological vision that undergirds this book. John has been a good friend and coworker during the past decade. John, I look forward to your coming books!

Appendix A

Sample Conversational Ground Rules

This appendix includes lists of ground rules from several communities as examples of conversational processes to which they commit themselves.

Silverton Friends is an Evangelical Friends congregation within the Northwest Yearly Meeting and is located in the small, rural town of Silverton, Oregon.

Consistent with our Quaker tradition, we believe God speaks in one voice, but we acknowledge that it often comes through many mouths. In order to practice working through challenging topics, we agree to the following:

1. We will embody the fruit of the Spirit: love, joy, peace, patience, kindness, goodness, faithfulness, gentleness, and self-control.

2. We will acknowledge Christ's presence among us and in each one of us.

3. We will practice empathy.

4. We will seek to understand above being understood.

5. We will wear a thick skin so others may express their authentic thoughts and feelings.

6. We will actively listen in love, suspending judgment.

7. We will be prepared to agree to disagree if necessary.

8. We will try not to ramble.

9. We will not play the role of know-it-all.

10. We will look for opportunities to find common ground.

11. We will lay down the need to persuade.

12. We will try not to be defensive, nor will we posture ourselves for the offense.

13. We will practice reconciliation.

14. We will not be afraid of silence.

MENNONITE CHURCH USA

The Mennonite Church USA has published a statement titled "Agreeing and Disagreeing in Love" that offers some ground rules for conversations around divisive topics. See an excerpt from the statement below.

"Making every effort to maintain the unity of the Spirit in the bond of peace" (Eph. 4:3), as both individual members and the body of Christ, we pledge that we shall:

1. Acknowledge together that conflict is a normal part of our life in the church (Rom. 14:1–8, 10–12, 17–19; 15:1–7).

2. Affirm that as God walks with us in conflict, we can work through to growth (Eph. 4:15–16).

3. Admit our needs and commit ourselves to pray for a mutually satisfactory solution (no prayers for my success or for the other to change but to find a joint way; James 5:16).

The full statement is available online at http://www.mennoniteusa .org/wp-content/uploads/2015/04/Agreeing-and-Disagreeing-in -Love_11-2013.pdf

MOUNTAIN LIFE CHURCH

Wednesday Morning Women's Group

Mountain Life Church in Park City, Utah, is affiliated with the Evangelical Free Church of America.

Based on Proverbs 18, our group has decided jointly to respect and love one another in our community by participating in the following group guidelines:

1. Confidentiality

    Anything that is discussed or prayed for in our group may not be shared outside of our time together. This will allow us to build trust and transparency with one another.

2. We will make every effort to come prepared and on time.

3. We desire to be encouraging, kind, compassionate, and sensitive.

4. We will be respectful, which means we will:

    a. Listen more than we speak.

    b. Discern when to speak and what is important to say. Be Spirit-led.

    c. Allow silence.

5. The primary purpose of the group is to study Scripture. We will stay focused and avoid digression (rabbit holes).

6. The facilitator may decide to limit a discussion for the sake of time or to keep a discussion on track.

SPRINGWATER COMMUNITY

Springwater Community is an intentional community in the Jesus tradition, located in the urban Lents neighborhood of Portland, Oregon.

Recognizing that at times in our life together we will have difficult group conversations, and desiring that these conversations conform us more deeply to the image of Christ, we agree to uphold and lovingly hold one another to the following agreements:

1. To mindfully schedule group conversations by allotting sufficient time, mitigating barriers to participation (such as childcare), and choosing a comfortable environment and time of day.

2. To intentionally prepare by appointing a facilitator to attend to procedure and keep the conversation on track, and by preparing ourselves as participants to engage the topic at hand.

3. To communicate clearly and honestly, speaking directly and taking responsibility for our words.

4. To cultivate a spirit of empathy by listening to understand, validating and reflecting what has been shared, welcoming and relating to others, and remaining attentive and engaged.

5. To foster our own openness and growth through curiosity, receptivity to the Spirit and trust in the Spirit's working in the group, focusing on interests rather than positions, acknowledging that I have things to offer and to learn, and allowing Scripture to open conversations.

6. To engage different modes of communication, utilize storytelling, and keep a sense of humor.

7. To honor equitable participation of those present, creating room for stakeholder voices, ensuring that decision-making is appropriate for the level of commitment, and allowing for a "free pass" when requested.

8. To mirror Christ's unconditional love, loving one another unconditionally in the midst of disagreements.

MARGARET WHEATLEY

Margaret Wheatley is a writer and management consultant who promotes the practice of conversation in the business environment. She is author of Turning to One Another: Simple Conversations to Restore Hope to the Future.[1]

I've learned to emphasize these principles before we begin a formal conversation process:

1. We acknowledge one another as equals.

2. We try to stay curious about each other.

3. We recognize that we need each other's help to become better listeners.

4. We slow down so we have time to think and reflect.

5. We remember that conversation is the natural way humans think together.

6. We expect it to be messy at times.

Appendix B

Additional Resources on Conversational Methods

Open Space Technology

Books

Owen, Harrison. *Expanding Our Now: The Story of OST*. San Francisco: Berrett-Koehler, 1997.

———. *Open Space Technology: A User's Guide*. San Francisco: Berrett-Koehler, 2008.

Online Resources

Herman, Michael. "Open Space Technology." MichaelHerman.com/cgi/wiki .cgi?OpenSpaceTechnology (a wealth of resources related to OST). OpenSpaceWorld.org.

Appreciative Inquiry

Books

Branson, Mark Lau. *Memories, Hopes, and Conversations: Appreciative Inquiry and Congregational Change*. Herndon, VA: Alban Institute, 2004.

Cooperrider, David, and Diana Whitney. *Appreciative Inquiry: A Positive Revolution in Change*. San Francisco: Berrett-Koehler, 2005.

Magruder Watkins, Jane, Bernard Mohr, and Ralph Kelly. *Appreciative Inquiry: Change at the Speed of Imagination*, 2nd ed. San Francisco: Pfeiffer, 2011.

Online Resources

AI Commons. "Introduction to Appreciative Inquiry." https://appreciativeinquiry.champlain.edu/learn/appreciative-inquiry-introduction.

The Center for Appreciative Inquiry. "What Is Appreciative Inquiry (AI)?" https://www.centerforappreciativeinquiry.net/more-on-ai/what-is-appreciative-inquiry-ai.

Elliott, Charles. *Locating the Energy for Change: An Introduction to Appreciative Inquiry*. International Institute for Sustainable Development. https://www.iisd.org/library/locating-energy-change-introduction-appreciative-inquiry.

World Café

Books

Brown, Juanita, and David Isaacs. *The World Café: Shaping Our Futures through Conversations That Matter*. San Francisco: Berrett-Koehler, 2005.

Online Resources

The World Café Community Foundation. "The World Café." TheWorldCafe.com.

www.TheWorldCafeCommunity.org.

Appendix C

Finding Common Ground in Conversations on Sexuality

Conversations about human sexuality and marriage are some of the most divisive that churches face today. In these conversations, we would do well to remind ourselves often of our unity in Christ and to find common ground on which those of diverse perspectives can agree. One of the earliest things that Grandview Calvary Baptist Church (Vancouver, BC) did in its conversations on sexuality was to create the following statement of common ground. I have included it here to stir our imaginations about how such conversations might move forward.

Common Ground to Stand On

In our discussion and discernment between 2009 and 2010, we gained some common ground. While we recognize that not every person in the church was able to adhere to the following beliefs, the council (pastors and deacons) at that time and the committee holding this process sought to develop and affirm some common ground that we could build on in our sexual ethics and practice.

Here are some truths we seek to affirm:

1. We are all created in the image of God, giving each of us inherent value and dignity.

2. Our sexuality is an integral part of our bodies and personhood. While our culture can reduce sexuality to having sex, sexuality has to do with how we relate to the world, with our longing for intimacy and being known, and with our need for human companionship.

3. Sexual desires are complex in origin and experience. A homosexual orientation may occur as a result of a combination of genes, prenatal hormones, and early childhood environment (as well as wounding in some cases). We acknowledge that discussions concerning the complex origin of sexual desires are sometimes hurtful and often unprofitable. We seek to be diligent in not judging or excluding one another based on who we desire or are attracted toward.

4. The historic teaching of the church is that the act of genital sex is ideally held within the covenant relationship of marriage between a man and a woman. The act of covenant is given to us in order to protect us from harm, in order to nurture bonds that take us deeper into the meaning of God's love, and in order to create a family where others can be welcomed and nurtured. A healthy sexuality is expressed in celibacy or covenantal commitment and in a community of love and accountability.

5. All of us are tainted by the fallenness of separation and resistance to God and God's ways, making us less than whole in our sexuality. Heterosexual and homosexual people are both tainted by this fallenness. For example, there is no evidence that homosexual people have a higher risk for abusing

children than heterosexual people do. We live in a culture that idolizes autonomy (doing our own thing apart from any authority or guide) and this plays itself out in our culture's resistance to the Biblical aims and boundaries around sex.

6. It is very difficult to change one's orientation from homosexual to heterosexual.

7. All those who respond to God's love in Christ are being redeemed and restored. Because the fullness of that restoration awaits the new creation, we live with imperfection and loss as well as joy and hope.

8. Our theological views and commitments around same-sex attraction and sexuality are important but not part of the essential teachings of the church (such as the divinity and humanity of Christ, the resurrection of Jesus, the hope of a new world, etc.).

Notes

Introduction: We Are Conversational Bodies

1. "The State of the Church 2016," Barna Group, September 15, 2016, https://www.barna.com/research/state-church-2016.

2. W. Daniel Hillis, "Edge Master Class 2010: W. Daniel Hillis on 'Cancering,'" Edge, December 27, 2010, https://www.edge.org/event/edge-master-class-2010-w-daniel-hillis-on-cancering.

3. Or perhaps, in cases such as in vitro fertilization, this intimate conversation would include others beyond our biological mother and father.

4. Robert Putnam, *Bowling Alone: The Collapse and Revival of American Community* (New York: Simon & Schuster, 2000), 27.

5. Bill Bishop, *The Big Sort: Why the Clustering of Like-Minded America Is Tearing Us Apart* (New York: Houghton Mifflin, 2008).

6. Brené Brown, *Braving the Wilderness: The Quest for True Belonging and the Courage to Stand Alone* (New York: Random House, 2017), 27.

Chapter 1: Orienting Ourselves for the Journey

1. Drawing on both the Nicene and Athanasian Creeds, philosopher Michael Rea articulates the three central, orthodox tenets of the doctrine of the Trinity: (1) There is exactly one God, whom the church has referred to historically as Father; (2) Father, Son, and Holy Spirit are not identical; (3) Father, Son, and Holy Spirit are of one substance (consubstantial). See Michael Rea, "The Trinity," in *The Oxford Handbook of Philosophical Theology*, ed. Thomas P. Flint and Michael Rea (Oxford: Oxford University Press, 2009), 405.

Even after more than two thousand years, the brightest theologians and philosophers still have not been able to offer a single, agreed-on account of the nature and operation of the Trinity. Recognizing this complicated history of wrestling to wrap our minds around the Trinity, I will not attempt to offer my own definitive account. Rather, I will draw on a particular interpretation of the Trinity, social trinitarianism, which—although it might have some philosophical challenges raised against it—provides an account of the Trinity that is compelling in this exploration of the practice of conversation.

2. "Who We Are," L'Arche USA, https://www.larcheusa.org/who-we-are.

3. Kristin Lin, "Community and the Complexities of Presence," *On Being* (blog), February 8, 2018, https://onbeing.org/blog/kristin-lin-community-and-the-complexities-of-presence.

4. Jean Vanier, "Long Road to Growth," *The Work of the People*, video, accessed March 30, 2018, http://www.theworkofthepeople.com/long-road-to-growth.

5. Christine Pohl, *Making Room: Recovering Hospitality as a Christian Tradition* (Grand Rapids: Eerdmans, 1999), 162.

6. Richard Unsworth, *A Portrait of Pacifists: Le Chambon, the Holocaust and the Lives of André and Magda Trocmé* (Syracuse, NY: Syracuse University Press, 2012), 175.

7. Rea, "Trinity," 405.

8. Chris Rice, *Grace Matters: A True Story of Race, Friendship, and Faith in the Heart of the South* (San Francisco: Jossey-Bass, 2002), 162.

9. "Our Covenant," Englewood Christian Church, July 2007, http://englewoodcc.com/covenant.html.

10. David Fitch, *Faithful Presence: Seven Disciplines That Shape the Church for Mission* (Downers Grove, IL: InterVarsity, 2016), 227.

11. Dallas Willard, "Salvation Is a Life," in *The Spirit of the Disciplines* (New York: Harper, 1988), 28–43.

12. "Dialogue of Salvation," in *Dialogue and Proclamation: Reflection and Orientations on Interreligious Dialogue and the Proclamation of the Gospel of Jesus Christ*, §38, Pontifical Council for Interreligious Dialogue, May 19, 1991, http://www.vatican.va/roman_curia/pontifical_councils/interelg/documents/rc_pc_interelg_doc_19051991_dialogue-and-proclamatio_en.html.

13. Willard, *Spirit of the Disciplines*, 19.

14. Fitch, *Faithful Presence*, 12.

15. Fitch, *Faithful Presence*, 36.

Chapter 2: Learning the Dynamics of Conversation

1. Gloria Galanes and Katherine Adams, *Effective Group Discussion: Theory and Practice*, 13th ed. (Boston: McGraw-Hill, 2010), 113.

2. Galanes and Adams, *Effective Group Discussion*, 112.

3. Roger Schwarz, *The Skilled Facilitator*, 2nd ed. (San Francisco: Jossey-Bass, 2002), 5.

4. Schwarz, *Skilled Facilitator*, 41.

5. Adapted from Schwarz, *Skilled Facilitator*, 137–40.

6. Schwarz, *Skilled Facilitator*, 267.

7. Here are some resources that your church might draw on to train facilitators: Ron Milam, "Facilitation Fundamentals," RonMilam.com, accessed February 22, 2018, https://ronpmilam.files.wordpress.com/2012/02/facilitationfundamentalsrev3.pdf (one-page handout); Schwarz, *Skilled Facilitator*; Sarah Campbell, *A Guide for Training Public Dialogue Facilitators* (East Hartford, CT: Paul J. Aicher Foundation, 2008), https://www.everyday-democracy.org/sites/default/files/attachments/Guide-Training-Public-Dialogue

-Facilitators_Everyday-Democracy.pdf; Office of Quality Improvement, University of Wisconsin–Madison, *Facilitator Tool Kit*, version 2.0 (Madison: University of Wisconsin System Board of Regents, 2007), https://oqi.wisc.edu/resourcelibrary/uploads/resources /Facilitator%20Tool%20Kit.pdf; Dale Hunter with Stephen Thorpe, Hamish Brown, and Anne Bailey, *The Art of Facilitation: The Essentials for Leading Great Meetings and Creating Group Synergy* (San Francisco: Jossey-Bass, 2009); Sam Kaner, *Facilitator's Guide to Participatory Decision-Making*, 3rd. ed. (San Francisco: Jossey-Bass, 2009); Ingrid Bens, *Advanced Facilitation Strategies: Tools and Techniques to Master Difficult Situations* (San Francisco: Jossey-Bass, 2005).

Chapter 3: What Will We Talk About?

1. "For Congregations (CFI [Congregational Formation Initiative])," Ekklesia Project, accessed January 22, 2018, http://www.ekklesiaproject.org/for-congregations-cfi. The CFI materials are organized in a multiyear process, but a congregation does not necessarily have to complete the whole process. However, given this intended order, a congregation would do well to start at the beginning of the CFI process, even if they don't plan to go all the way through it.

2. Philip Kenneson, Debra Dean Murphy, Jenny C. Williams, Stephen E. Fowl, and James W. Lewis, *The Shape of Our Lives*, Getting Your Feet Wet 1 (Eugene, OR: Wipf & Stock, 2008), 4.

3. Philip Kenneson, Debra Dean Murphy, Jenny C. Williams, Stephen E. Fowl, and James W. Lewis, *The Shape of God's Reign*, Getting Your Feet Wet 2 (Eugene, OR: Wipf & Stock, 2008), 4.

4. I explore the crucial role of reading in helping us work better and more faithfully in my book *Reading for the Common Good: How Books Help Our Churches and Neighborhoods Flourish* (Downers Grove, IL: InterVarsity, 2016), esp. chaps. 4–6.

5. Jean Vanier, *Community and Growth*, rev. ed. (New York: Paulist Press, 1989), 122–23.

6. John Erik Pattison, "Book Club: The Church, the Bible, and the LGBTQ Community," August 20, 2015, http://johnepattison.com/bookclub-church-bible-lgbtq.

Chapter 4: The Healing Potential of Conversational Methods

1. Harrison Owen, "Opening Space for Emerging Order," Open Space World, accessed November 22, 2017, http://www.openspaceworld.com/brief_history.htm.

2. Harrison Owen, *Open Space Technology: A User's Guide* (San Francisco: Berrett-Koehler, 2008), 70. Owen's four principles are not given in an ordered list, and I have presented them in a different order than they appear in his book.

3. Owen, *Open Space Technology*, 95.

4. Michael Herman, "Talking about Open Space," MichaelHerman.com, June 22, 2016, http://www.michaelherman.com/cgi/wiki.cgi?TalkingAboutOpenSpace.

5. David Cooperrider and Diana Whitney, *Appreciative Inquiry: A Positive Revolution in Change* (San Francisco: Berrett-Koehler, 2005), 8.

6. Mark Lau Branson, *Memories, Hopes, and Conversations: Appreciative Inquiry and Congregational Change* (Herndon, VA: Alban Institute, 2004), 28.

7. Branson, *Memories, Hopes, and Conversations*, 29.

8. Branson, *Memories, Hopes, and Conversations*, 104.

9. Branson, *Memories, Hopes, and Conversations*, 68–69.

10. Branson, *Memories, Hopes, and Conversations*, 73.

11. Branson, *Memories, Hopes, and Conversations*, 96.

12. Branson, *Memories, Hopes, and Conversations*, 108.

13. Juanita Brown and David Isaacs, *The World Café: Shaping Our Futures through Conversations That Matter* (San Francisco: Berrett-Koehler, 2005), 15.

14. Brown and Isaacs, *World Café*, 15.

15. "Third way" is a descriptor used for churches that are neither affirming of same-sex marriage nor nonaffirming. For an introduction, see Jonathan Merritt's interview with Wendy VanderWal-Gritter, "A Third Way for Christians on the 'Gay Issue?'," Religion News Service, August 11, 2014, https://religionnews.com/2014/08/11/third-way-christians -gay-issues.

16. Lucas Land, Facebook direct message to author, November 21, 2017.

Chapter 5: Conversation as a Prayerful Way of Being

1. Philip Kenneson, *Practicing Ecclesial Patience: Patient Practice Makes Perfect* (Eugene, OR: Ekklesia Project, 2013), 10.

2. Henri Nouwen, *The Way of the Heart: Desert Spirituality and Contemporary Ministry* (New York: Seabury, 1981), 46.

3. Martin Buber, *Between Man and Man* (New York: Macmillan, 1965), 7.

4. Brent Bill, *Holy Silence: The Gift of Quaker Spirituality* (Brewster, MA: Paraclete, 2012), 7.

5. Michael Birkel, *Silence and Witness: The Quaker Tradition* (Maryknoll, NY: Orbis, 2004), 40.

6. Joy Banks, email message to author, February 28, 2018.

7. Nouwen, *Way of the Heart*, 57.

8. Henri J. M. Nouwen, Donald P. McNeill, and Douglas A. Morrison, *Compassion: A Reflection on the Christian Life*, rev. ed. (New York: Image, 2006), 93.

9. See, for instance, https://blacklivesmatter.com/about/.

Chapter 6: Abiding in the Messiness of Life

1. See, e.g., Rom. 8:26; 1 Cor. 1:25–27; 2 Cor. 11:30; 12:9–10. Marva Dawn has done some excellent theological reflection on weakness in her book *Joy in Our Weakness: A Gift of Hope from the Book of Revelation*, rev. ed. (Grand Rapids: Eerdmans, 2002).

2. George Ritzer, *The McDonaldization of Society: An Investigation into the Changing Character of Contemporary Social Life* (Los Angeles: Sage, 2012), 13–15. Note that Ritzer refers to quantifiability as calculability, but I have used the former term here as its meaning might be clearer for the nonacademic readers of this book.

3. Kenneson, *Practicing Ecclesial Patience*, 5.

4. Nouwen, McNeill, and Morrison, *Compassion*, 93.

5. Episcopal Church, *Book of Common Prayer and Administration of the Sacraments and Other Rites and Ceremonies of the Church* (New York: Church Pension Fund, 1945), 301.

6. Gerald Schlabach, *Unlearning Protestantism: Sustaining Christian Community in an Unstable Age* (Grand Rapids: Brazos, 2010), 89.

7. Nouwen, McNeill, and Morrison, *Compassion*, 80–81.

8. Lesslie Newbigin, *Proper Confidence: Faith, Doubt, and Certainty in Christian Discipleship* (Grand Rapids: Eerdmans, 1995), 66–67.

9. Newbigin, *Proper Confidence*, 66–67.

10. Newbigin, *Proper Confidence*, 66.

Chapter 7: Preparing Our Whole Selves for Conversation

1. "Our Covenant," Englewood Christian Church, July 2007. Available online at http://englewoodcc.com/covenant.html.

2. Richard Foster, *Celebration of Discipline: The Path to Spiritual Growth* (San Francisco: Harper, 2002), 162.

3. Foster, *Celebration of Discipline*, 163.

4. Kenneson, *Practicing Ecclesial Patience*, 10.

5. The following are just a few important books on the benefits of Sabbath and rest: Walter Brueggemann, *Sabbath as Resistance: Saying No to the Culture of Now* (Louisville: Westminster John Knox, 2014); Marva Dawn, *Keeping the Sabbath Wholly: Ceasing, Resting, Embracing, Feasting* (Grand Rapids: Eerdmans, 1989); Alex Soojung-Kim Pang, *Rest: Why You Get More Done When You Work Less* (New York: Basic Books, 2016); Matthew Sleeth, *24/6: A Prescription for a Healthier, Happier Life* (Carol Stream, IL: Tyndale, 2012); Norman Wirzba, *Living the Sabbath: Discovering the Rhythms of Rest and Delight* (Grand Rapids: Brazos, 2006).

Chapter 8: Cultivating a Sense of Mission and Identity

1. Woodrow Wilson, "Address Delivered at Joint Session of the Two Houses of Congress," April 2, 1917; US 65th Congress, first session, Senate Document 5.

2. Tyler Wigg-Stevenson, *The World Is Not Ours to Save: Finding the Freedom to Do Good* (Downers Grove, IL: InterVarsity, 2013), 35–38.

3. "Agents of memory" is a phrase borrowed from John Howard Yoder's paper "The Hermeneutics of Peoplehood," in *The Priestly Kingdom: Social Ethics as Gospel* (South Bend, IN: Notre Dame, 1985).

4. Wendell Berry, *Remembering* (Berkeley: Counterpoint Press, 2008).

5. Tato Sumantri, Facebook direct message to author, February 28, 2018.

Chapter 9: Sustaining Conversation through Conflict

1. Vanier, *Community and Growth*, 120.

2. David Janzen, "Conflict," in *Called to Community: The Life Jesus Wants for His People* (Walden, NY: Plough, 2016), 193.

3. Olli-Pekka Vainio, *Disagreeing Virtuously: Religious Conflict in Interdisciplinary Perspective* (Grand Rapids: Eerdmans, 2017), 158.

4. Vainio, *Disagreeing Virtuously*, 165.

5. Vainio, *Disagreeing Virtuously*, 167.

6. David Janzen, *The Intentional Christian Community Handbook* (Brewster, MA: Paraclete, 2013), 114.

7. Janzen, *Intentional Christian Community Handbook*, 286.

Chapter 10: Enmeshing Ourselves in the Dance of Community

1. Justin B. Fung, "Eugene Peterson on the Trinity," September 22, 2016, https://www.justinbfung.com/2016/09/22/eugene-peterson-on-the-trinity. Fung recounts the story from a 2016 speaking event that Peterson did.

2. For example, Dwight Friesen, Tim Soerens, and Paul Sparks, *The New Parish* (Downers Grove, IL: InterVarsity, 2014); John Pattison and C. Christopher Smith, *Slow Church* (Downers Grove, IL: InterVarsity, 2014); and Michelle Ferrigno Warren, *The Power of Proximity* (Downers Grove, IL: InterVarsity, 2017).

3. Willie James Jennings, "Thinking Theologically about Space: An Interview with Willie James Jennings, *The Englewood Review of Books* 1, no. 1 (Advent 2010): 4–6.

4. Parts of this section have been adapted from my book *Reading for the Common Good: How Books Help Our Churches and Neighborhoods Flourish* (Downers Grove, IL: IVP Books, 2016), 74–76.

Conclusion: Conversational Bodies Bearing Witness

1. David Dark, *Life's Too Short to Pretend You're Not Religious* (Downers Grove, IL: InterVarsity, 2016), 22.

Appendix A: Sample Conversational Ground Rules

1. Margaret Wheatley, *Turning to One Another: Simple Conversations to Restore Hope to the Future* (San Francisco: Berrett-Koehler, 2009), 33.

About the Author

C. Christopher Smith is a writer, community developer, and editor of *The Englewood Review of Books*. He is coauthor of the award-winning book *Slow Church: Cultivating Community in the Patient Way of Jesus* and the author of *Reading for the Common Good: How Books Help Our Churches and Neighborhoods Flourish*. His work has been featured in the *Washington Post*, *USA Today*, the *Indianapolis Star*, *HuffPost*, *Christianity Today*, the *Christian Century*, *Relevant*, and *Sojourners*. Smith lives on the urban Near Eastside of Indianapolis, Indiana, where he is a longtime member of Englewood Christian Church, a congregation that has been learning to talk together for over two decades.

THE ENGLEWOOD
Review of Books